KNOCKOUT

THE ULTIMATE GUIDE TO SUCKER PUNCHING

DROP HIM WITH JUST ONE PUNCH!

SAMMY FRANCO

Also by Sammy Franco

Kubotan Power: Quick & Simple Steps to Mastering the Kubotan Keychain
The Heavy Bag Bible
The Widow Maker Compendium
Invincible: Mental Toughness Techniques for Peak Performance
Bruce Lee's 5 Methods of Attack
Unleash Hell: A Step-by-Step Guide to Devastating Widow Maker Combinations
Feral Fighting: Advanced Widow Maker Fighting Techniques
The Widow Maker Program: Extreme Self-Defense for Deadly Force Situations
Savage Street Fighting: Tactical Savagery as a Last Resort
Heavy Bag Workout
Heavy Bag Combinations
Heavy Bag Training
The Complete Body Opponent Bag Book
Stand and Deliver: A Street Warrior's Guide to Tactical Combat Stances
Maximum Damage: Hidden Secrets Behind Brutal Fighting Combinations
First Strike: End a Fight in Ten Seconds or Less!
The Bigger They Are, The Harder They Fall
Self-Defense Tips and Tricks
Gun Safety: For Home Defense and Concealed Carry
Out of the Cage: A Guide to Beating a Mixed Martial Artist on the Street
Warrior Wisdom: Inspiring Ideas from the World's Greatest Warriors
War Machine: How to Transform Yourself Into a Vicious and Deadly Street Fighter
1001 Street Fighting Secrets
When Seconds Count: Self-Defense for the Real World
Killer Instinct: Unarmed Combat for Street Survival
Street Lethal: Unarmed Urban Combat

Knockout: The Ultimate Guide to Sucker Punching

ISBN: 978-1-941845-32-5
Printed in the United States of America

Published by Contemporary Fighting Arts, LLC.
Visit us Online at: **SammyFranco.com**
Follow him on Twitter: **@RealSammyFranco**

For author interviews or publicity information, please send inquiries in care of the publisher.

Dedication

For Achilles, my best friend and loyal companion who never left my side. A beautiful, high-spirited German Shepherd who brought out the kid in me each and every day. Until we meet again, my heart will remain broken.

"When danger is imminent, strike first, strike fast, strike hard, and keep the pressure on."

– Sammy Franco

Contents

Caution!

The self-defense techniques, tactics, methods, and information described and depicted in this book can be dangerous and could result in serious injury and or death and should not be used or practiced in any way without the guidance of a qualified reality based self-defense instructor.

The author, publisher, and distributors of this book disclaim any liability from loss, injury, or damage, personal or otherwise, resulting from the information and procedures in this book. This book is for academic study only.

Before you begin any exercise program, including those suggested in this book, it is important to check with your physician to see if you have any condition that might be aggravated by strenuous exercise.

Remember, it's your sole responsibility to research and comply with all local, state and federal laws and regulations pertaining to the application of self-defense techniques.

About This Book

Knockout is a one-of-a-kind book designed to teach you the lost art and science of sucker punching in a self-defense situation.

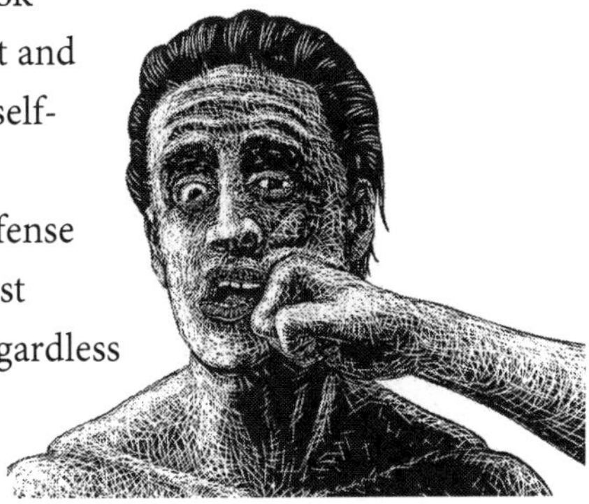

Sucker punching is a self-defense skill that can be performed by just about anyone, young and old, regardless of size or strength or level of experience. Most importantly, you don't need martial arts training to master these simple and effective fighting techniques.

Some readers might wonder how this book differs from the principles outlined in my previous book, ***First Strike: End a Fight in Ten Seconds or Less.*** Knockout is an offshoot of my first strike principle, and it focuses exclusively on the tricks, ruses, and deceptions that facilitate an effective sucker punch.

Unlike other self-defense books, Knockout is devoid of tricky or flashy fighting moves that can get you injured or possibly killed when defending against a determined attacker. Instead, it arms you with practical and deceptive fighting techniques that work in the chaos of real-life street assaults. In fact, the skills and techniques found in these pages are surprisingly simple and easy to apply.

Beware, the information and techniques contained herein are dangerous and should only be used to protect yourself or a loved one from the immediate risk of unlawful injury. Remember, the decision to throw a sucker punch must always be a last resort, after all other means of avoiding violence have been exhausted.

Practitioners who regularly practice the skills and techniques featured in this book will establish a rock solid foundation for using sucker punching for personal defense. Moreover, the techniques featured in this book will significantly improve your overall self-defense skills, enhance your conditioning, and introduce you to a new and exciting method of personal protection.

Knockout is based on my 30+ years of research, training and teaching the martial arts and combat sciences. In fact, I've taught these unique fighting skills to thousands of my students, and I'm confident they can help protect you and your loved ones during a time of need.

Knockout has seven chapters, each one covering a critical aspect of training. Since this is both a skill-building workbook and training guide, feel free to write in the margins, underline passages, and dog-ear the pages.

Finally, I encourage you to read this book from beginning to end, chapter by chapter. Only after you have read the entire book should you treat it as a reference and skip around, reading those chapters that directly apply to you.

Good luck in your training!

Sammy Franco

Chapter 1
Anatomy of a Sucker Punch

What is a Sucker Punch?

In the broadest sense of the term, a sucker punch is a sudden blow delivered without warning to an unsuspecting victim. Since the blow is unexpected, the recipient isn't prepared to defend himself against the unforeseen attack.

Sucker punches are most commonly delivered with the fists. In fact, the two most common blows that are thrown are the right overhand and haymaker punch. However, more advanced forms of sucker punching (including those discussed in this book) might include:

- **Head and throat strikes**
- **Elbow strikes**
- **Weapons**
- **Power Amplifiers**
- **Environmental exploitation tactics**
- **Partner assisted set-ups**

Finally, depending on the situation, a sucker punch can be executed from the front, side and behind the unsuspecting recipient.

The sucker punch is not just limited to street fighting. In fact, there are documented instances where the sucker punch has been used in professional boxing.

A punch with a bad reputation

Of all the hand-to-hand fighting techniques know to man, sucker punching is by far the most controversial. Because of its unconventional and deceitful way of defeating the adversary, many consider sucker punching a cowardly way of fighting. In fact, it's often referred to as a "cheap shot", "coward punch", and "bitch move".

To make matters even worse, street criminals will often use the sucker punch to efficiently incapacitate their victims before robbing them, while there are others who will use it for their own sick amusement.

Take, for example, the infamous and disturbing "knockout game," where one or more assailants will try to knock out a random unsuspecting victim. Even more disturbing is the fact that these attacks are often videotaped by the accomplices for entertainment purposes. Indeed, we live in a very sick world!

Why you need sucker punching skills

Notwithstanding its bad reputation and propensity for criminal abuse, sucker punching is a valid self-defense option for law abiding citizens. In fact, it's an essential part of a reality based street survival training. Here are several compelling reasons why you should consider mastering the art of sucker punching.

The "knockout game" is no game at all. Serious injuries and even deaths have been attributed to this heinous crime.

1. It minimizes your chances of injury or death

Every self-defense situation needs to be won fast. Remember, the longer a fight lasts, the greater your chances of serious injury or even death. Every technique and tactic that you apply in a fight must be efficient, effective and provide the least amount of danger and risk.

Sucker punching is one of the best methods of achieving these three objectives because it allows you to incapacitate your assailant swiftly while, at the same time, negating his ability to retaliate. As a result, no time is wasted, and no unnecessary risks are taken.

2. He who hits first, often wins the fight

In most fights, if you don't initiate the first strike, your adversary most likely will. Allowing the opponent the opportunity to deliver the first punch is extremely dangerous. It's like allowing a gunslinger to draw his weapon first. If he's a good shot, you are done!

In hand-to-hand fighting, if you allow the assailant to strike you first, he might injure or possibly kill you, and he will most certainly force you into an irreversible series of defensive moves that will inhibit you from issuing an effective counterattack.

3. It's difficult to recover from a sucker punch

There's an old saying, "*The hardest punch, is the one you never see coming.*" Truer words have never been spoken, especially when it comes to the art and science of sucker punching.

There's much more to sucker punching than just slugging the guy in the face. In fact, it's a delicate mixture of science and art, psychology and warfare.

The element of surprise is invaluable in a fight, and the sucker punch is the quintessential surprise attack that instantly gives you a substantial advantage over your adversary.

Sucker punching gives you the upper hand by allowing you to quickly overwhelm your opponent's mind and body. In other words, you demolish his defenses and take him out of the fight.

4. It's a great equalizer during an unfair fight

A properly placed sucker punch can defeat anyone, regardless of their size or strength. This is especially important when you are confronted with a larger and stronger adversary who is determined to harm you.

Nothing can be more dangerous than defending against multiple attackers. Fortunately, sucker punching is an essential survival technique when faced with such a perilous situation.

In fact, in my e-book titled **The 10 Best Ways to Defeat Multiple Attackers**, I discuss the vital importance of sucker punching the leader or *alpha* of the pack first. In many instances, he's the one who controls the spirit of the group and motivates the others to attack.

Because of the extreme threat and danger posed by multiple assailants, it is essential to make an example of the leader by severely injuring or crippling him. For example, if the others accomplices see their buddy violently choking from a sucker punch strike to the throat, they'll be less inclined to continue their assault on you.

Sucker punching is not just limited to fisted blows. There are several open hand strikes that can do serious damage to your adversary. More will be discussed in Chapter 4.

Sucker punching is an essential survival technique when faced with multiple attackers.

5. It protects you from being victimized

In order to prevent being victimized by a sucker punch, you must know how to apply it yourself. In essence, you must understand the nature of the beast. You've got to open your ears, eyes, and mind to the many techniques, tactics, strategies of the street criminal or barroom brawler. This will greatly enhance your ability to avoid such attacks and, beyond that, to deal with a particular attack if it occurs.

The Real Concerns of Sucker Punching

Unfortunately, there are some inherent concerns that come with sucker punching. Being aware of these issues will better prepare you to deal with it, should it arise. Let's take a look at some of them.

1. Spectator intervention is possible

Most people are inveterate supporters of the underdog: they just hate to see anyone lose a fight. Witness or spectator intervention is a common occurrence during a street fight, especially if you sucker punch someone. Therefore, when attacking you adversary, be cognizant and leery of all spectators in your immediate surrounding There's no telling what they might do after witnessing a sucker punch attack.

2. Moral, emotional or religious issues

Let's be clear, sucker punch requires a particular type of psychological and emotional makeup - it's not for everyone! It demands an offensive mentality that compels you to act rather than react. It requires you to be aggressive and take affirmative and absolute control of the situation by making all the decisions and acting immediately without apprehension or trepidation.

Unfortunately, many self-defense and martial arts instructors teach their students to wait for their opponent to make the first move. Frankly, it's a big mistake that can cost you dearly in a fight. In the real world, this reactive type of approach can get you seriously injured or possibly killed.

There are also people who are simply too timid to take the initiative and hit first. For some people, there are religious and philosophical beliefs that prohibit them from throwing a sucker punch in a fight. Many won't strike first because they simply don't know how to execute a sucker punch successfully. Others are

If you plan on delivering a sucker punch in front of other people, try to place yourself close to an escape route. Escape routes can include windows, doors, fire escapes, gates, bridges, staircases, fences, escalators, or any other avenue that will allow you to flee quickly and safely from the scene.

uncertain about the legal requirements and justifications, and, as a result, they second-guess their instincts, hesitate, and end up kissing the pavement.

Therefore, it's imperative that you have a basic understanding of the legal requirements of launching a sucker punch in a self-defense situation. More will be discussed in Chapter 2.

3. You might accidentally kill him

Sucker punching has been known to kill people. But how is that possible? After all, its just a punch to the head.

As I have stated in some of my other books, any punch has the potential to kill your assailant. It's just a matter of the target you hit and the amount of force you apply to that particular target. Take, for example, a strike delivered to the opponent's throat. A direct and powerful strike to this target may result in unconsciousness, blood drowning, massive hemorrhaging, strangulation, and death.

Notwithstanding the vulnerabilities of the human anatomy, a properly delivered sucker punch will most likely knock your opponent unconscious. However, the danger occurs when his body drops to the ground and his head hits a hard surface like concrete or asphalt. Unfortunately, in some cases, it's the head injury from the fall that leads to death.

On the streets, there is no bushido, the honorable code of the ancient warrior. There are no rules of combat etiquette. Real life situations of violence are bloody, unpredictable, and extremely dangerous.

4. You can get sued or land in jail

The most difficult aspect of sucker punching is determining exactly when you can hit first. Well, since every self-defense situation is going to be different, there is no simple answer. However, there are some fundamental elements that must be present if you are going to throw a sucker punch.

First, you must never use force against another person unless it is absolutely justified. Force is broken down into two levels: lethal and nonlethal. Lethal force is defined as the amount of force that can cause serious bodily injury or death. Nonlethal force is an amount of force that does not cause serious bodily injury or death.

Keep in mind that any time you use physical force against another person, you run the risk of having a civil suit filed against you. Anyone can hire a lawyer and file a suit for damages. Likewise, anyone can file a criminal complaint against you. Whether criminal charges will be brought against you depends upon the prosecutor's or grand jury's view of the facts.

Second, sucker punching should only be used as an act of protection against unlawful injury or the immediate risk of unlawful injury. If you decide to sucker punch your adversary, you'd better be damn certain that a reasonable threat exists and that it is absolutely necessary to protect yourself from immediate danger. Remember, sucker punching has to be a last resort, after all other means of avoiding violence have been exhausted.

Finally, you must change your perspective and acknowledge sucker punching as both a legitimate and proactive form of self-defense. In other words, a sucker punch should be viewed as the strategic application of proactive force designed to interrupt the initial stages of an assault before it becomes a self-defense situation.

In addition, whenever you are threatened by a dangerous adversary and there is no way to escape safely, you must strike first, strike fast, strike with authority, and keep the pressure on. This offensive strategy is known as my first-strike principle, and it's essential to the process of neutralizing a formidable adversary in a self-defense altercation.

By the time the adversary knows he's been hit by your sucker punch, there's no time for him to prepare for the series of blows that follow.

Chapter 2
Things You Should Know

Sucker Punch Concepts and Principles

Before we get down to the nitty-gritty details of pucker sucking, you're going to need to understand a few important concepts that establish the foundation for a knockout punch. These concepts include the following:

- **Sucker punch stages**
- **Sucker punch ranges**
- **Sucker punch assessments**

Let's start by discussing the two different stages of sucker punching.

The Two Sucker Punch Stages

In order to effectively deliver a sucker punch in a fight, it's important to understand the two different stages of conflict and how they relate to the successful deployment of a first strike. Essentially, the two stages or phases are:

- **Precontact Stage**
- **Contact Stage**

A successful sucker punch requires you to exploit both the precontact and contact stages of fighting.

The Precontact Stage of Sucker Punching

The precontact stage of sucker punching refers to the few critical moments before you actually hit your assailant. During this phase, you will *manipulate* your adversary by employing a variety of verbal and nonverbal techniques to set him up for your attack. However, to pull this off you must always be in complete control of yourself, both physically and emotionally.

Some of these precontact techniques will include disingenuous vocalization, non-threatening body language, and strategic positioning. All of these cunning concepts and deceptive ruses will be discussed in greater detail in Chapter 3.

Pictured here, the precontact stage of sucker punching.

Sucker punching is the art of "psychologically manipulating" the aggressor by using both verbal and nonverbal techniques to set him up for your attack.

The precontact stage is the *most critical period* because it's when you soften the opponent up for your attack. In the moments before your strike, the opponent is truly unaware of the impending danger and is caught off guard when your punch hits its intended target.

The Contact Stage of Sucker Punching

The contact stage is when you strike your adversary. This is often delivered in the form of a punch, but can be delivered by other means. In Chapter 4, I'll teach you some of the best sucker punch techniques that will drop your opponent without fail.

Pictured here, the contact stage of sucker punching.

Sucker Punch Ranges

Before you can successfully deliver your attack, you must understand range or distancing. Range is the spatial relationship between you and your adversary.

When assessing your opponent, you'll need to recognize the strategic implications and advantages of his range. For example, is he close enough to land a sucker punch effectively? Or is he at a distance from which he could effectively evade your blow?

In hand-to-hand fighting, for example, there are three possible ranges from which your can launch an attack: kicking, punching, and grappling. Let's take a look at each one.

The kicking range

The farthest distance of unarmed combat is kicking range. At this distance you are usually too far away to strike with your hands, so you use your legs to strike your opponent.

Pictured here, the kicking range.

Kicking techniques can always be used as a back up if your sucker punch fails to meet its mark. However, if you are going to execute kicking techniques in a fight, always employ low-line kicks to targets below the assailant's waist.

Unfortunately, since the opponent is several feet away from you, the kicking range is not an ideal place to launch a sucker punch. While kicking techniques do have their place in self-defense, they are simply inefficient for sucker punching applications.

The punching range

Punching range is the midrange of unarmed fighting. At this distance, you are close enough to the opponent to strike him with your hands and fists.

At this distance sucker punch techniques are quick, efficient, and effective, and they include the finger jab, palm heel, hook, uppercut, web-hand strike, and hammer fist. I'll be discussing the specific striking techniques in Chapter 4.

The punching range.

The grappling range

The third and closest range of unarmed combat is grappling range. At this distance, you are too close to your opponent to kick or execute most long range hand strikes, so you would use close-quarter techniques to incapacitate your adversary.

Grappling range is divided into two different planes: horizontal and vertical. For our purposes, we are only going to focus on the vertical plane, which permits you to deliver elbow strikes and head butts. Like the punching distance, vertical plane grappling range also permits effective sucker punching techniques.

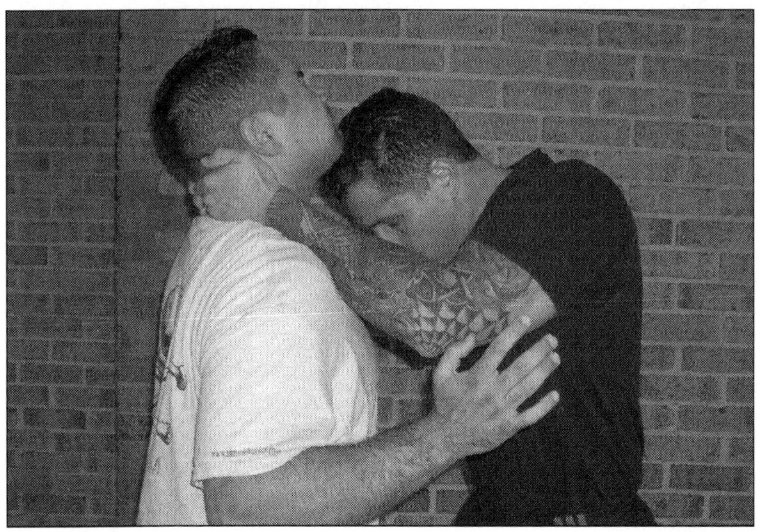

The grappling range.

The Neutral Zone

The neutral zone is the distance at which neither you nor your opponent can strike one another. Although the neutral zone is the ideal place to be when assessing your environment and your

In the event you are not prepared to deliver a sucker punch, the neutral zone can also be used temporarily to keep you out of harm's way.

adversary, it's the wrong place to be when attempting to throw a sucker punch. Remember, in order to initiate a sucker punch, you must be standing in either the punching or grappling range of unarmed combat.

The neutral zone.

Sucker Punch Assessments

Unless you want to spend some time in jail, you must be certain that your actions are justified in the eyes of the law. As I mentioned in Chapter 1, you must never use force against another person unless it is absolutely justified. Sucker punching should only be used as an act of protection against unlawful injury or the immediate risk of unlawful injury.

Again, if you decide to sucker punch your opponent, you'd better be certain that a reasonable threat exists and that it is absolutely necessary to protect yourself from immediate danger.

Does a reasonable threat exist?

To determine whether a reasonable threat exists, you must assess your self-defense situation accurately. Assessment is the process of rapidly gathering and analyzing information and then accurately evaluating it in terms of threat and danger. In general, there are two things to assess prior to launching a sucker punch: the environment and the individual. Let's start with the environment and its related elements.

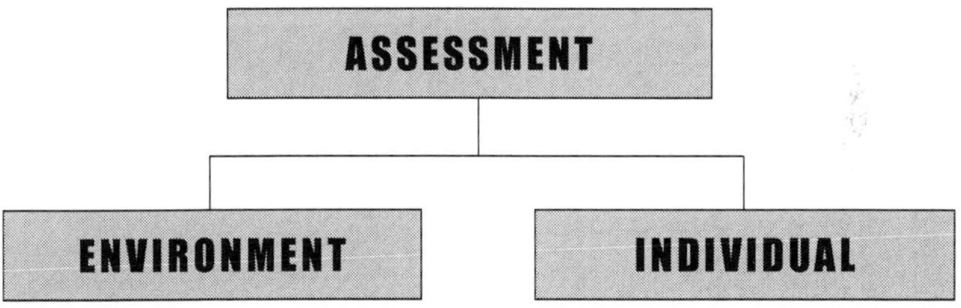

The Environment

Before delivering a sucker punch, you must strategically evaluate your environment, which is made up of your immediate surroundings. It can be a parking lot, your car, your bedroom, your office, an airport, a park, elevator, nightclub, movie theater, etc.

However, there are four essential factors to consider when assessing your environment. They are escape routes, barriers, make-shift weapons, and terrain. Let's take a look at each one.

In chapter 6, I discuss a variety of different ways you can exploit your immediate environment to gain the tactical advantage over your adversary.

1. Escape routes. These are the various avenues or exits from a threatening situation. There is nothing cowardly about running away from a dangerous situation, especially if you're outnumbered. The ultimate goal of self-defense is to survive. Some possible escape routes are windows, doors, fire escapes, gates, escalators, fences, walls, bridges, and staircases. But be careful that your version of an escape route doesn't lead you into a worse situation.

2. Barriers. A barrier is any object that obstructs the attacker's path of attack. At the very least, barriers give you distance and some precious time, and they may give you some temporary safety from your adversary.

A barrier must have the structural integrity to perform the particular function you have assigned it. Barriers are everywhere and include such things as large desks, doors, automobiles, dumpsters, large trees, fences, walls, heavy machinery, and large vending machines. The list is endless and depends on the situation, but it is a good idea to assess in advance any possible barriers when entering a potentially hostile or dangerous environment.

Your environment plays an important role in the outcome of a fight.

3. Makeshift weapons. These are common, everyday objects that can be converted into offensive and defensive hand-held weapons. Like a barrier, a makeshift weapon must be appropriate to the function you have assigned to it. For instance, you won't be able to knock someone out with a car antennae, but you could whip it across their eyes and temporarily blind them. Whereas you could knock someone unconscious with a good heavy flashlight but you could not use it to shield yourself from a knife attack.

4. Terrain. This is a critical environmental factor. What are the strategic implications of the terrain that you are standing on? Will the surface area interfere with your ability to throw an effective sucker punch? Is the terrain wet or dry, mobile or stationary? Obviously, if you are standing on ice, you will be restricted in your efforts to quickly escape or attempt full-force power strikes. If the surface is moving, like an escalator, for example, you may be required to avoid using sucker punch techniques altogether.

The Individual

Obviously, in a potentially dangerous situation, you need to assess the source of the threat. Who is posing the possible danger? Is it someone you know or is he a complete stranger? Is it one person or two or more? What are his or her intentions in confronting you? Don't forget to pay attention to all available clues, particularly verbal and nonverbal indicators.

Let all five of your senses go to work to absorb the necessary information. Also don't forget to listen to what your gut instincts are telling you about the threatening person(s). There are five essential factors to consider when assessing a threatening individual: demeanor, intent, range, positioning, and weapon capability.

1. Demeanor. In the broadest terms we are talking about the individual's outward behavior. Watch for clues and cues. Is he shaking, or is he calm and calculated? Are his shoulders hunched or relaxed? Are his hands clenched? Is his neck taut? Are his teeth clenched? Is he breathing hard? Does he seem angry or frustrated, or confused and scared? Does he seem high on drugs? Is he mentally ill or simply intoxicated? What is he saying? How is he saying it? Is his speech slurred? What is his tone of voice? Is he talking rapidly or methodically? Is he cursing and angry? All of these verbal and nonverbal cues are essential in assessing the individual's overall demeanor and thus adjusting your sucker punch strategy accordingly.

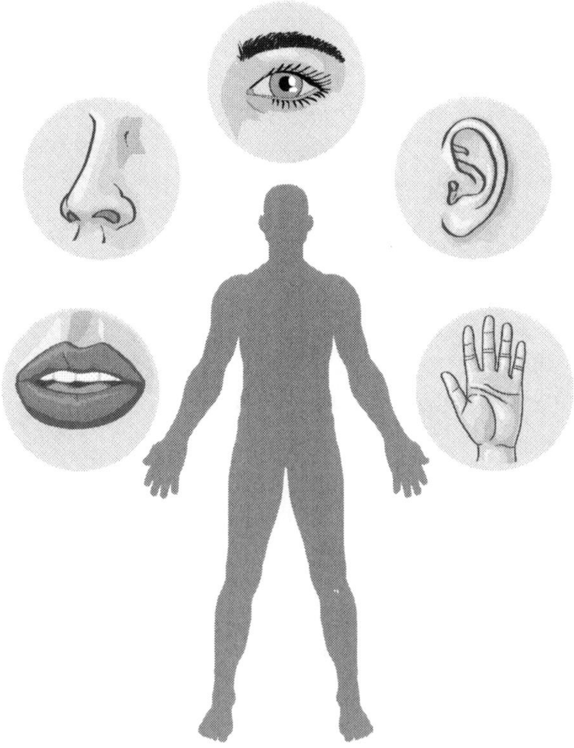

When assessing your adversary, let all of your five senses go to work to absorb all the necessary information.

2. Intent. Once you've got a good read on the assailant's demeanor, you're in a much better position to assess his or her intent. In other words, just what is this person's purpose in confronting or threatening you? Does he intend to rob you? Is he seeking retribution for something you have done? Or is he simply looking to pick a fight with you?

Determining the individual's intent is perhaps the most important assessment factor, but it can also be the most difficult. Moreover, when it comes to criminal intent, things can change pretty fast. For example, an intent to intimidate you can quickly turn into an intent to assault. In any event, the appropriate tactical response is highly dependent upon a correct assessment of intent.

3. Range. As I stated earlier, range is the spatial relationship between you and the assailant(s) in terms of distance. In self-defense there are three possible distances from which your assailant can launch an attack:

- **Kicking range**
- **Punching range**
- **Grappling range**

When assessing a threatening individual, you'll need to recognize the strategic implications of his range. For example, how close is he from launching an effective attack? Is he at a distance from which he could kick you? Is he in a range that allows him to grab hold of

Properly assessing a threatening opponent will also allow you to select the appropriate level of force for your situation. This is particularly important when delivering a legally justified sucker punch.

you, take you to the ground, or cut you with an edged weapon? Is he moving through the ranges of unarmed combat? If so, how fast? Does he continue to move forward when you step back?

4. Positioning. This is the spatial relationship of the assailant(s) to you in terms of threat, escape, and target selection. Are you surrounded by multiple assailants or only one? Is he standing squarely or sideways, above or below you? What sucker punch targets does the assailant present you with? Is he blocking the door or any other avenue of escape? Is his back to the light source? Is he close to your only makeshift weapon? You must answer these questions before choosing a tactical strategy appropriate to the situation.

5. Weapon capability. Is your assailant armed or unarmed? If he is carrying a weapon, what type is it? Does he have a delivery method for the particular weapon? Is he armed with more than one weapon? Sometimes it is easy to determine if someone is armed. For example, you see a knife sheath on his belt. At other times your assessment

Just because you can't see a weapon, doesn't mean it's not there.

skills need to be more advanced. For instance, is the person wearing a jacket when it is too hot for a jacket? Could it be to conceal a gun at the waist? Is the person patting his chest? When scanning the person, can you see his hands and all his fingertips? Is one hand behind him or in his pockets? Could he be palming a knife or some other edged weapon? Are his arms crossed? Does he seem to be reaching for something? Does he seem suspiciously rooted to a particular spot? Is his body language incongruous with his verbal cues you are reading?

Chapter 3
The Set-Up

The Most Important Aspect of Sucker Punching

In this chapter, I'm going to teach you the most important aspect of sucker punching - the Set-Up. Delivering a knockout punch requires a unique mixture of science and art. In fact, seventy-five percent of an effective sucker punch is the initial set-up, while the remaining twenty-five percent is the actual strike.

What's Included in the Set-Up

The set-up includes a variety of tactics and techniques that help exploit and manipulate your adversary in order to maximize the successful delivery of your first strike. This includes some of the following:

- **The Delivery System**
- **Psychological Manipulation**
- **Environmental Exploitation**
- **Sucker Punch Ruses**

The effective delivery of a sucker punch requires that all four of these set-up ingredients work in tandem with one another. In this chapter, I will address each component of the set-up except sucker punch ruses, which will be covered in great length in Chapter 6.

The Set-Up requires both verbal and nonverbal tactics to manipulate your adversary into the ideal sucker punch position.

The Sucker Punch Delivery System

If you want to improve the odds of successfully landing your sucker punch, you'll need a delivery system that will maximize the efficiency and effectiveness of your strike. This means you'll need to master some important stances. When I say *stances* I am referring to a strategic posture you assume prior to and during a fight. There are three:

- **De-escalation Stance**
- **Natural Stance**
- **Fighting Stance**

Let's take a look at each one and see how they are used in a sucker punch situation.

The De-escalation Stance

So what is de-escalation and why is it important for sucker punching? De-escalation is the strategic process of diffusing a potentially violent confrontation. The goal is to eliminate the possibility of an agitated individual resorting to physical violence.

De-escalation requires you to use both verbal and nonverbal techniques to calm the hostile person, while employing tactically deceptive physical safeguards to create the appearance that you are totally non aggressive. It is the art of "tactically calming" the aggressor. You must be in total control of yourself, both physically and emotionally in order to deal effectively with someone on the verge of losing control.

By mastering my de-escalation stance, you will greatly enhance your capability to diffuse the escalating dynamics of a hostile confrontation. At the same time, however, you'll be prepared to deliver a devastating sucker punch, if necessary.

When de-escalating an irate individual, you must remember to keep your cool. If you lose control, show fear, or express frustration or anger, you will only make matters worse.

De-escalation Stance Characteristics

The de-escalation stance is used exclusively during the precontact stage of self-defense and there are two variations that you will need to learn. They are:

- **De-escalation Stance (punching range)**
- **De-escalation Stance (grappling range)**

De-escalation Stance (punching range)

This stance is used when you are faced with an opponent in the punching range of unarmed combat. Let's begin by taking a closer look at the specific components of this strategic stance.

The Head

When assuming this de-escalation stance, keep your head straight and focused directly at your adversary. Try to keep your chin slightly angled down. This diminishes target size and reduces the likelihood of a paralyzing blow to the chin or a lethal strike to the throat. However, it's also very important that you appear nonthreatening and uncombative to your adversary.

The Torso

The centerline of your torso should be strategically positioned at a 45-degree angle from your adversary. When assuming the de-escalation stance, place your strongest, most coordinated side forward. For example, a right-handed person stands with his or her right side toward the assailant. Keeping your strongest side forward enhances the speed, power, and accuracy of your sucker punch. This doesn't mean that you should never practice from your other side. You must be capable of de-escalating from both sides, and you should spend equal practice time on the left and right stances.

The Lead and Rear Arms

Keep your hands open, relaxed and up to protect the upper portion of your centerline. Never drop your hands to your side, put your hands in your pocket, or cross your arms. You've got to have your hands up to protect your targets and, if necessary, to deliver a powerful sucker punch. Don't point your finger or clench your fists! Keep your hands loosely open, both facing the hostile person.

The De-escalation Stance (punching range)

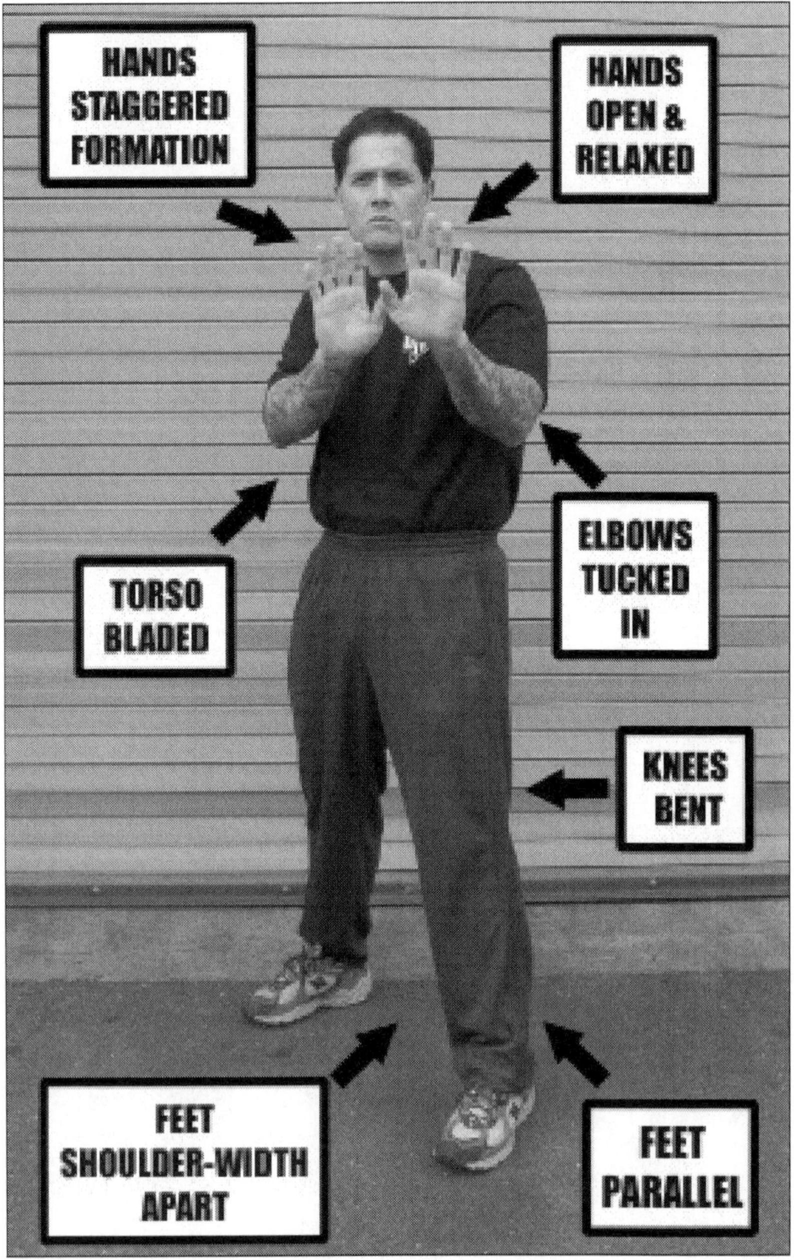

The hands are generally placed one behind the other in a staggered formation along your centerline. The lead arm is held high and bent at approximately 90 degrees. The rear arm is kept back. Arranged this way, the hands not only protect the torso centerline but also allow quick deployment of your sucker punch. Finally, when holding your hand guard, do not tighten your shoulder or arm muscle. Stay relaxed and loose.

The Lead and Rear Legs

When assuming your de-escalation stance, place your feet about shoulder width apart. Keep your knees bent and flexible. Your weight distribution is also an important factor. Since self-defense is

Left de-escalation stance for punching range (side view).

Right de-escalation stance for punching range (side view).

dynamic, your weight distribution will change frequently. However, when stationary, keep 50 percent of your body weight on each leg and always be in control of it.

When assuming the de-escalation stance for punching range, try to place one hand behind the other in a staggered formation.

De-escalation Stance (grappling range)

This variation of the de-escalation stance is used when you are confronted by an opponent in the grappling range of unarmed combat. I often jokingly refer to grappling range as the "bad breath range" because the opponent intentionally encroaches your personal space.

The Head

Like the other de-escalation stance, you want to keep your head straight with your chin slightly angled down. Remember, you must always appear nonthreatening and uncombative to your adversary.

Keep both of your eyes focus on your threatening adversary but avoid direct and steady eye contact with the hostile person. A quick glance every so often is okay, but avoid becoming transfixed. It is too risky and dangerous for you. First, the hostile person may interpret direct eye contact as challenging or threatening. Second, the aggressor's eyes can also psyche you out or project false intentions. While the eyes may be windows to the soul, they provide no vital information about your assailant's possible attack. Therefore, as a general rule of thumb, I recommend focusing your gaze between the assailant's mouth and throat region and letting your peripheral vision take in the person's shoulders and torso, like that of a triangle.

The Torso

Since both of your shoulders are facing squarely in front of your opponent, you'll be forced to expose your torso centerline. This is unavoidable. However, since you're in such close proximity to the adversary, there's no need to be concerned about being hit with linear punches (i.e., jabs, rear crosses, etc). The distance will negate their effectiveness.

Fanning you fingers out when de-escalating often indicates fright and is also a good way to get one of your fingers broken or sprained.

The De-escalation Stance (grappling range)

Once again, when assuming the de-escalation stance, try to place your strongest, most coordinated side forward. For example, a right-handed person stands with his or her right side toward the assailant. Keeping your strongest side forward enhances the speed, power, and accuracy of your sucker punch (this is assuming it's legally and morally justified in the eyes of the law).

Right lead de-escalation stance for grappling range.

Left lead de-escalation stance for grappling range.

The Lead and Rear Arms

Both of your arms are held up, side by side, with your hands open and relaxed. Again, never drop your hands to your side, put your hands in your pocket, or cross your arms. You've got to have your hands up to strategically protect your anatomical targets and, if necessary, to strike first with a deceptive sucker punch.

The Lead and Rear Legs

When assuming your stance, place your feet about shoulder width apart. Keep your knees bent and flexible. Your weight distribution is also an important factor. Since street fighting is dynamic, your weight distribution will change frequently. However, when stationary, keep 50 percent of your body weight on each leg and always be in control of it.

The grappling range de-escalation stance requires you to place both of your hands side by side.

One of the most common mistakes made with the de-escalation stance is the tendency to curl your finger inward. This type of clawing configuration looks aggressive and threatening, which defeats the entire purpose of your stance.

Another common mistake is to fan your fingers out. This hand articulation indicates alarm or fright to the adversary.

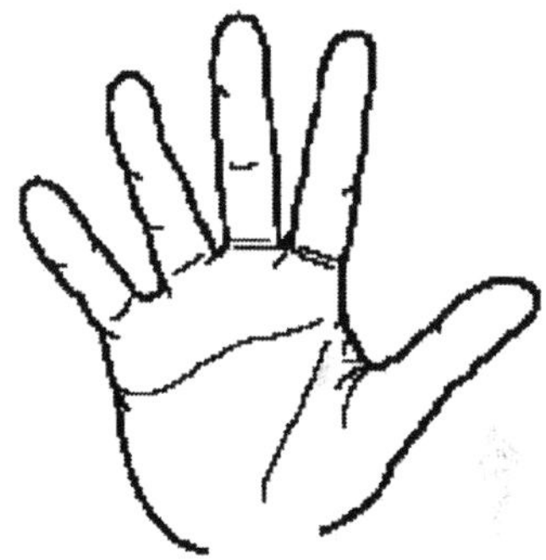

Here is an example of the correct way to hold your hands. Notice that both of your hands are open, relaxed, and up to protect the upper portion of your centerline.

Psychological Implications of the De-escalation Stance

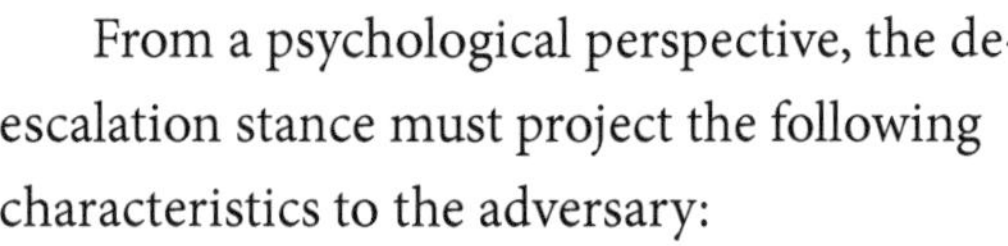

The de-escalation stance, by itself, is not enough, In fact, it must be used in conjunction with both verbal and nonverbal techniques designed to psychologically manipulate a hostile person. The goal is to employ tactically deceptive physical safeguards to create the appearance that you are totally non aggressive. Remember, de-escalation is the art of "tactically calming" the aggressor.

From a psychological perspective, the de-escalation stance must project the following characteristics to the adversary:

1. **You must appear non aggressive** - The de-escalation stance is the complete antithesis of combat mode, requiring you to appear non aggressive to your opponent. When a threatening person observes your stance, he should immediately perceive you as peaceful. This also applies to your voice. For example, when confronting a hostile person, you must remove all threatening aspects from your voice. Always maintain a tone of voice that is friendly, concerned, and nonthreatening.
2. **You must appear cooperative** - You also want to convince a threatening person that you are cooperative and willing to compromise. So watch out for words or verbal commands like "relax," "calm down," "shut up," "stay back," "don't move," "keep your distance," or "cool out." Such phrases often provoke hostility and anger. Don't make any threats like "if you get any closer, you'll regret it," "if you touch me you're

gonna get it," or "don't make me hurt you. It's better to use phrases as "hey, I'm really sorry," "please, let's talk this out," or "I can understand your anger." Get into the habit of saying "excuse me," "pardon me," or "oops, my fault" when someone bumps into you.

De-escalation requires you to be in total control of yourself, both physically and emotionally in order to deal effectively with someone on the verge of losing control. Pictured here, the de-escalation stance used in grappling range.

The de-escalation stance can also have a positive impact on your own attitude and behavior during the hostile encounter. However, this requires that the following requirements are met.

1. **It must evoke restraint** - The de-escalation stance should immediately transform your mind and body to the highest levels of personal restraint. You must be in total control of yourself, both physically and emotionally in order to deal effectively with someone on the verge of losing control. Remember, if you are not part of the solution, you will be

part of the problem.

2. **It must feel comfortable** - Your de-escalation stance must also feel physically comfortable. When assuming the posture, it must immediately create a mental and psychological comfort zone that will allow you to deal with a barrage of emotional hostility. Remember, if your stance feels uncomfortable, then now is the time to change it so it works with you in a time of need.
3. **You must feel savvy** - The de-escalation stance must empower you. It should make you feel like a smart and tactically savvy technician who can rise above the ego's trappings by taking the moral high ground. This is especially important when dealing with a verbally hostile person who attempts to threaten, browbeat, or intimidate you.

De-escalation Stance Overview

- Used during the precontact stages of self-defense.
- You must always appear non-aggressive and cooperative.
- When in punching range, your torso centerline is positioned at 45 degrees from opponent.
- When in grappling range, both hands positioned side by side with torso centerline facing the opponent.
- Strongest side of body faces adversary.
- Shoulders and arms are relaxed but ready.
- Elbows point down to the ground.
- 50% percent weight distribution on both legs.
- Knees are bent, flexible, and ready.
- Feet set approximately shoulder width apart.

Reconciling De-escalation and Sucker Punching: The Gemini Principle

Before you launch your sucker punch, there is almost always going to be some form of dialogue between you and the opponent. This is when the ***Gemini Principle*** should be used.

The Gemini principle is the strategic and deceptive use of both verbal and nonverbal skills that enables you to successfully launch a preemptive strike. As in the Gemini zodiac, you need to summon the dark twin of your persona to effectively perform this type of disingenuous behavior.

Once you assume your de-escalation stance, your next objective is to psychologically manipulate or soften your adversary by speaking to him in a calm and unresisting tone of voice, telling him that you have no intentions of fighting. *The key is to prolong the opponent's thought process and momentarily distract him.* Once he takes the bait and lowers his guard, deliver your sucker punch and keep the pressure on until he is thoroughly incapacitated (generally the best time to strike your opponent is while you're talking to him, preferably in the form of a question).

This form of disingenuous vocalization requires a calm demeanor, precise timing, and a good bit of acting on your part. When conducting the Gemini Principle be certain not to get locked into a heated or argumentative dialogue with your adversary. Remember, dialogue is just another sucker punch tool that is used to slacken an opponent's defenses and provide you with a window of opportunity.

WARNING: Like any tactic or strategy, the Gemini principle can backfire if not properly and confidently employed. You'll need to regularly practice these techniques to ensure they will work for you when you need them.

De-escalation Stance Drill (Chest Push)

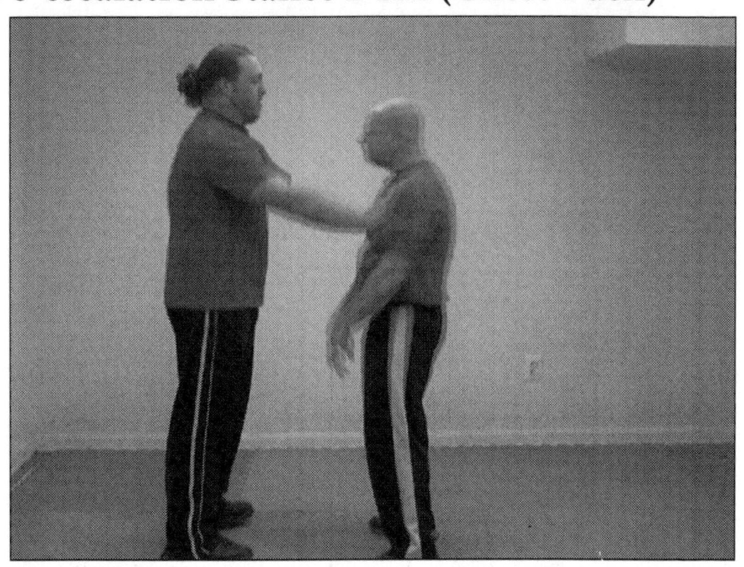

The chest push drill is a great exercise that will accomplishes the following four training objectives.

1. It teaches you to reflexively assume a de-escalation stance when being shoved or pushed by your opponent.
2. It develops the ability to quickly recover your balance when suddenly being pushed.
3. It toughens your body and conditions your nervous system to withstand the shock of a jolting chest push. Believe it or not, many people are unaccustomed to this type of contact and often freeze.
4. It conditions your emotions NOT to react with an immediate counter attack. From a tactical standpoint, the worst time to counter your adversary is immediately after he pushes you. This is when he will most expects it. The objective is to learn to maintain emotional calm and retaliate only at the ideal moment.

STEP 1: Begin by standing face-to-face with your training partner.

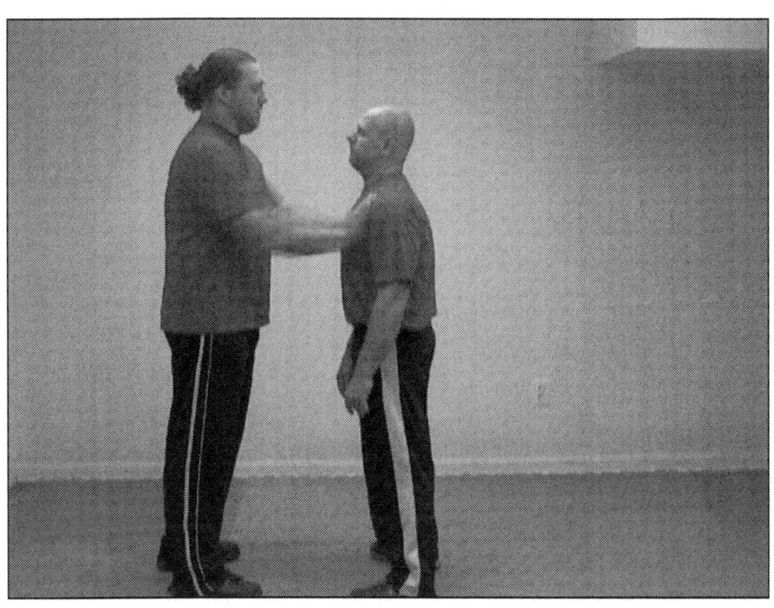

STEP 2: The drill begins with your partner stepping forward and shoving you.

STEP 3: Take the full effect of the push.

STEP 4: Quickly recover your balance and raise both of your hands up.

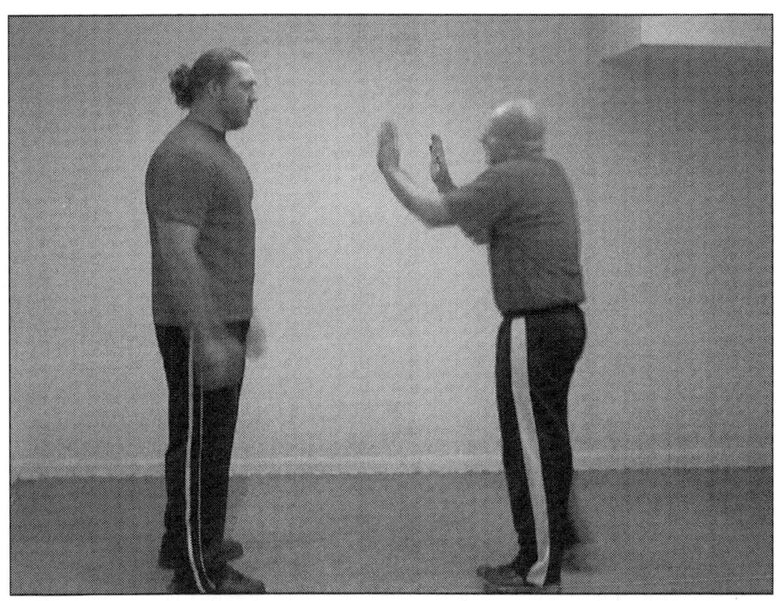

STEP 5: Try to assume a de-escalation stance.

STEP 6: Step back and verbally diffuse the situation.

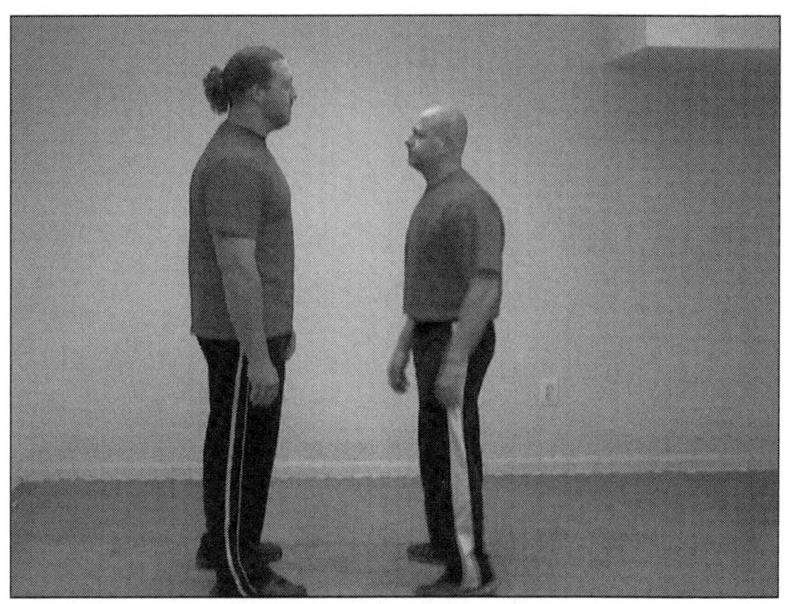

STEP 7: Next, walk up to your partner.

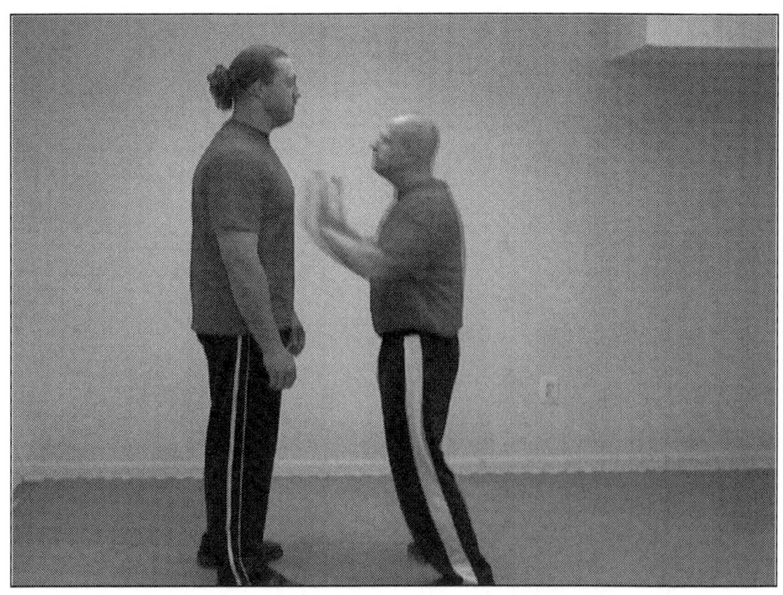

STEP 8: Begin the drill again by pushing him forcefully against his chest.

STEP 9: Avoid tensing your muscles and absorb the full effect of the push.

STEP 10: Let the momentum of the push throw you backwards.

STEP 11: Quickly regain your balance and assume a de-escalation stance.

STEP 12: Try to verbally diffuse the threat.

De-escalation Stance Drill (Mirror Scenarios)

One of the best ways to develop and refine your de-escalation stance is to practice in front of a mirror. To begin, stand in front of a full-length mirror and picture a de-escalation scenario in your mind.

Envision a very angry and hostile person screaming at you. Once this scenario is crystal clear, assume the proper de-escalation stance and look into the mirror.

Now, assess your stance while being cognizant of your physiology and hand positioning. Next, speak out loud and verbally defuse the situation with this imaginary hostile person. Remember to always use selective semantics (choice words) for your scenario.

To evaluate your performance, you may want to videotape the exercise. There are hundreds of possible de-escalation scenarios to practice. Here are a few to get you started:

1. Angry bar patron
2. Disgruntled employee
3. Angry spouse
4. Resentful relative
5. Irate customer or client

6. Drunken friend
7. Enraged motorist
8. Unbalanced street vagrant
9. Egotistical punk
10. Jealous or suspicious friend
11. Confrontation neighbor
12. Irate or emotionally fueled protester
13. Quarrelsome religious fanatic
14. Argumentative street vendor
15. Mentally ill family member
16. Racist verbal assault
17. Overzealous sports fanatic

Always remember that a stance is a luxury in a self-defense situation. There might be some situations that don't allow you the time or opportunity to assume a strategic posture.

The Natural Stance

The natural stance is another strategic posture used during the precontact stages of self-defense. Essentially, the natural stance is used when you're face to face with a person and you are not sure of their true intentions. For example, lets say you are standing at a street corner waiting for the bus, when suddenly you are approached by a stranger asking for directions. In this situation, you're not certain if this stranger is innocently asking for assistance or if he's possibly setting you up for an attack.

In the above example, it's important to utilize some type of protective posture in the event that he has nefarious intentions. The natural stance is the ideal posture to assume when faced with such a situation because it appears innocuous, yet it permits effective sucker punching capability.

As a general rule of thumb, when dealing with strangers on the streets, it's best to keep moving and avoid any type of conversation.

The natural stance requires you to always keep your hands up.

However, there are some instances when you don't have the option to simply walk away and go about your business. For example, if you were waiting for a bus, or taxi or meeting friends at a specified location.

If you must stop and briefly talk with a stranger on the street, the natural stance will provide you with numerous tactical advantages. As a matter of fact, for many years I worked as a bouncer in several bars in Washington, DC and I used the natural stance frequently when "working the door." The natural stance allowed me to conduct business with some very unsavory patrons without tipping them off that I was prepared to possibly defend and counter attack. So if shit hit the fan (as it often did), I would always be ready and able to respond accordingly.

Natural Stance Characteristics

The Head

When assuming the natural stance, keep your head straight and focused directly at your adversary. The goal is to appear relaxed and at ease, hence the name -***natural stance.*** Also, keep both of your eyes focus on the stranger when communicating with him and avoid locking eyes. Once again, a quick glance every so often is okay, but avoid becoming transfixed.

The Torso

The centerline of your torso should be strategically positioned at a 45-degree angle from your adversary. When assuming a natural stance, place your strongest, most coordinated side forward. For example, a right-handed person stands with his or her right side toward the assailant. Keeping your strongest side forward enhances the speed, power, and accuracy of your first strike. This doesn't mean that you should never practice from your other side. You must be

The Natural Stance

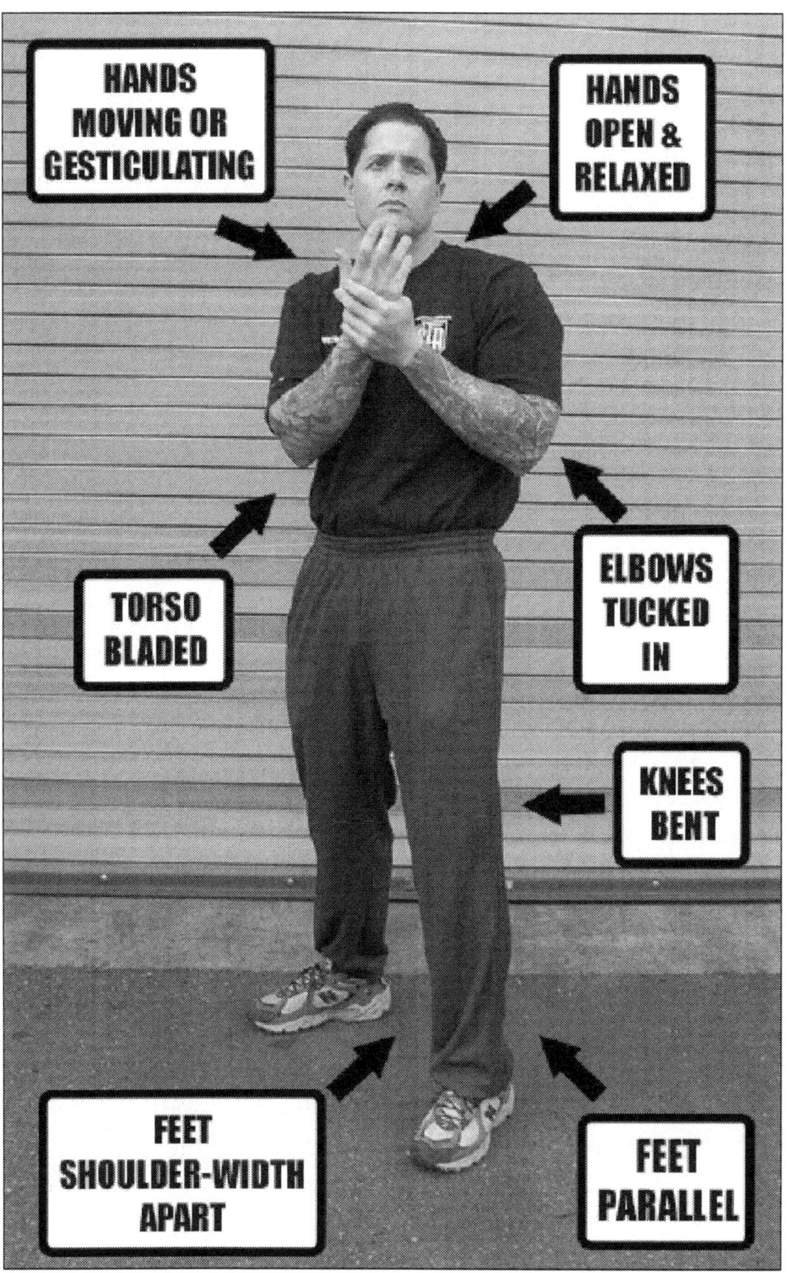

capable of fighting from both sides, and you should spend equal practice time on the left and right stances.

The Lead and Rear Arms

Both of your hands must always remain up and moving. The goal is to keep them moving in a natural manner. For example, you can rub your hands, scratch you elbows, chest, hands or face. Just remember to make it look natural. A good rule of thumb is to get into the habit of gesticulating when talking to strangers. This type of constant hand movement is beneficial for numerous reasons:

1. It masks the defensive nature of your hands being raised at all times.
2. It helps set up your sucker punch (if morally and legally justified).
3. It helps improve the speed of both offensive and defensive technique by preventing inertia from setting in.
4. It masks hand trembling that often occurs during the precontact stages of unarmed combat.
5. It aids in communication skills.

The Lead and Rear Legs

When assuming your natural stance, place your feet about shoulder width apart. Keep your knees bent and flexible. Think of your legs as power springs to launch you through the ranges of unarmed self-defense.

All footwork and strategic movement should be performed on the balls of your feet. Your weight distribution is also an important factor. Since self-defense is dynamic, your weight distribution will change frequently. However, when stationary, keep 50 percent of your body weight on each leg and always be in control of it.

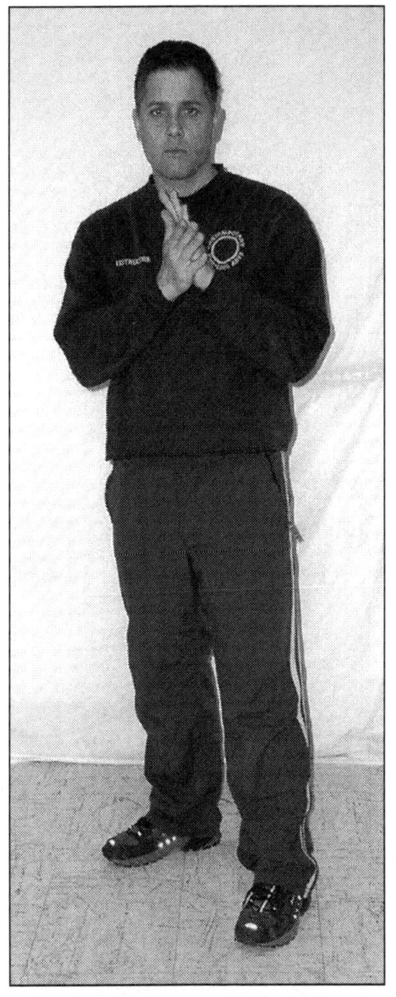

The natural stance - rubbing the hands.

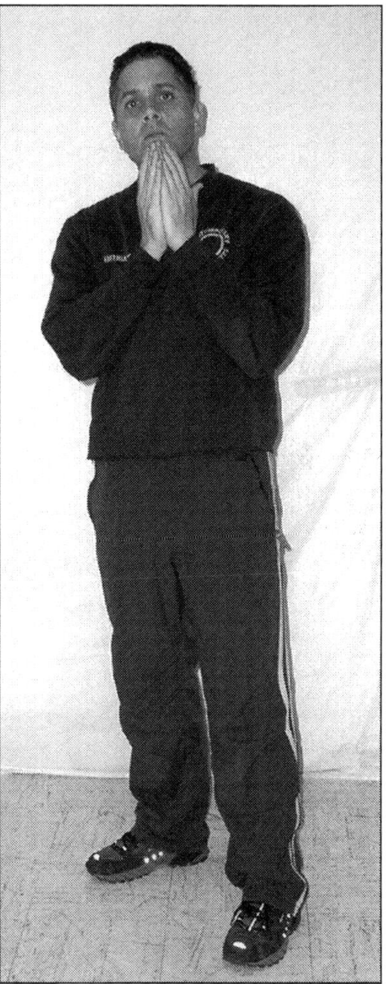

The natural stance - hands on chin.

A good rule of thumb is to get into the habit of gesticulating when talking to any stranger. This type of constant hand movement is beneficial for numerous strategic reasons.

The natural stance - scratching the head.

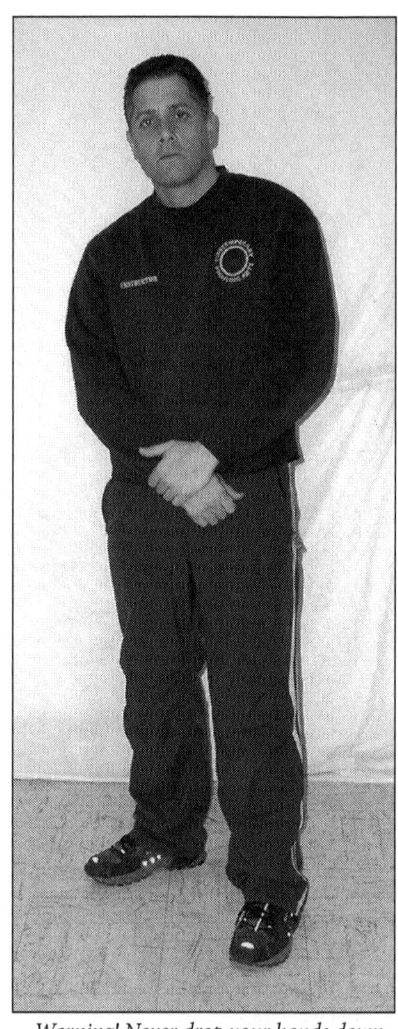
Warning! Never drop your hands down to your waist. This is a quick way to get knocked out.

Psychological Implications of the Natural Stance

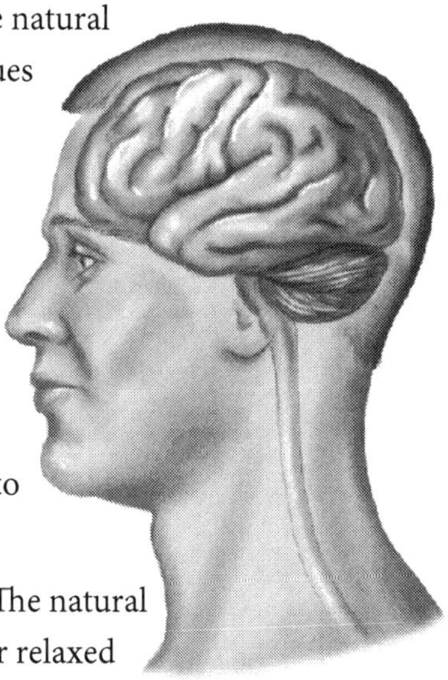

Like the de-escalation stance, the natural stance will utilize nonverbal techniques to psychologically dupe a potentially dangerous person. Once again, the objective is to employ deceptive physical safeguards to create the appearance that you are relaxed and aware. From a psychological perspective, the natural stance must project the following characteristics to the individual:

1. **You must appear relaxed** - The natural stance requires you to appear relaxed and calm. If you appear anxious or tense, you will immediately project this to the individual causing you to lose the tactical advantage.
2. **You must appear aware** - You also want to appear alert, assertive, and purposeful to the stranger. This actually acts as a deterrent to a criminal looking for an easy mark to attack. Remember, seasoned criminals love to attack people who appear weak, fearful, distracted, or preoccupied.

The natural stance can also have a positive impact on your own attitude and behavior. However, this requires that the following requirements are met.

1. **It must feel comfortable** - Like all combat stances, this one must also feel physically comfortable. When assuming this posture, you should feel relaxed and at ease, but always ready. Remember, if your stance feels awkward or rigid, then change or modify it so it can still maintain some of its tactical

properties.

2. **You must feel savvy** - The natural stance should empower you, making you feel like a smart and tactically savvy technician who can match wits with a criminal predator. This is especially true when dealing with seasoned criminals who want to "size you up" before launching his own sucker punch.

Natural Stance Overview

- Used during the precontact stages of fighting.
- Used when you're uncertain of a stranger's true intentions.
- Your torso centerline is positioned at 45 degrees from the individual.
- Hands are always up, moving or gesticulating.
- Strongest side of body faces adversary.
- Shoulders and arms are relaxed but ready.
- Elbows point down to the ground.
- 50% percent weight distribution on both legs.
- Knees are bent, flexible, and ready.
- Feet set approximately shoulder width apart.
- Your face and body must look relaxed and at ease.

Natural Stance Drill (Side Stepping)

Here is a great drill that will improve your ability to side step an attack from the natural stance position. This exercise is also important for refining evasion skills and for enhancing your sense of range and timing.

To practice the sidestepping drill, employ the following:

1. Begin with your training partner standing approximately eight feet from you.
2. Assume a natural stance.
3. Without telegraphing his intentions, your training partner should charge at you full-speed.
4. If you're standing in a right natural stance, quickly step with your right foot to the right and have your left leg follow an equal distance. Your partner should miss you and you should be balanced and ready to effectively counterattack.
5. Practice the sidestepping drill at various distances, in different lighting conditions, and while standing on different surfaces.

The Fluidity of Stances

The following photo sequence demonstrate how several different stances can be used in the course of a single self-defense altercation. Pictured here, the man on the right assumes a natural stance when confronted by a stranger.

The man (left) becomes aggressive and pushes the defender.

The defender employs a punching range de-escalation stance and begins diffusing the situation.

The assailant steps closer and the defender adjusts to a grappling range de-escalation stance.

The Fighting Stance

The third and final stance you'll need to know is called the fighting stance and it's used in the event that your sucker punch doesn't immediately put an end to the fight. For example, let's say your preemptive punch misses its intended target and now you're faced with an enraged opponent. In this situation, you are going to need a fighting stance that will allow you to apply both offensive and defensive techniques.

The fighting stance that I am going to teach you should only be used when you're physically fighting an unarmed assailant. Meaning, it is strictly designed for unarmed encounters when combat is already taking place. *It should not be used during the precontact stages of combat or during armed encounters with a knife, bludgeon, or gun.* Finally, never launch a sucker punch from a fighting stance, doing so will eliminate the element of surprise.

This fighting stance defines your ability to execute your natural body weapons and techniques, and it will play a material role in the outcome of a self-defense situation.

The fighting stance also maximizes both your offensive and defensive capabilities. It stresses strategic soundness and simplicity over complexity and style. The fighting stance facilitates optimum execution of your body weapons while simultaneously protecting your vital body targets against quick counter strikes.

The fighting stance can also serve as a reference point when training. For example, when I teach my students both offensive and defensive techniques, it generally comes from the reference point of a fighting stance. As a matter of fact, in just about all of my books, the reader will see techniques demonstrated from a fighting stance.

The fighting stance can also be used when there is a brief pause in combat engagement. For example, after delivering a sucker punch, you'll want to disengage the fight but remain ready to re-engage, if

The fighting stance serves a vital role when training. For example, the practitioner will almost always assume a fighting stance before and after launching a punching combination.

necessary. Again, this would be conducted from a fighting stance.

Like I said before, the fighting stance should not be used during the precontact stages of a fight. As a matter of fact, very seldom will a smart self-defense technician square off with his adversary in a fighting stance. While this may be popular in Hollywood movies and video games, it's the wrong approach for the real world self-defense.

However, this is not to say that it doesn't happen. It actually does occur. For example, in the many years that I worked as a bouncer, I've seen mixed martial artists and boxers (who are untrained for precontact combat scenarios) assume fighting stances before blows are exchanged in a street fight. Unfortunately, this unsophisticated approach eliminates numerous tactical and strategic advantages.

Now that you have a general understanding of when you would use a fighting stance, let's talk about some of its important characteristics.

Fighting Stance Characteristics

The Head

One of the most important elements of your fighting stance is your head position. A poorly positioned head can easily lead to a broken nose, concussion, knockout, or fractured windpipe.

When assuming your fighting stance, keep your head slightly angled down with both of your eyes focused directly at your

When assuming a fighting stance, avoid the tendency to lower your hand guard, which leaves you wide open to a possible counterattack. Remember, when executing a punch or strike, keep your other hand up to either defend or follow up with another strike.

The Fighting Stance

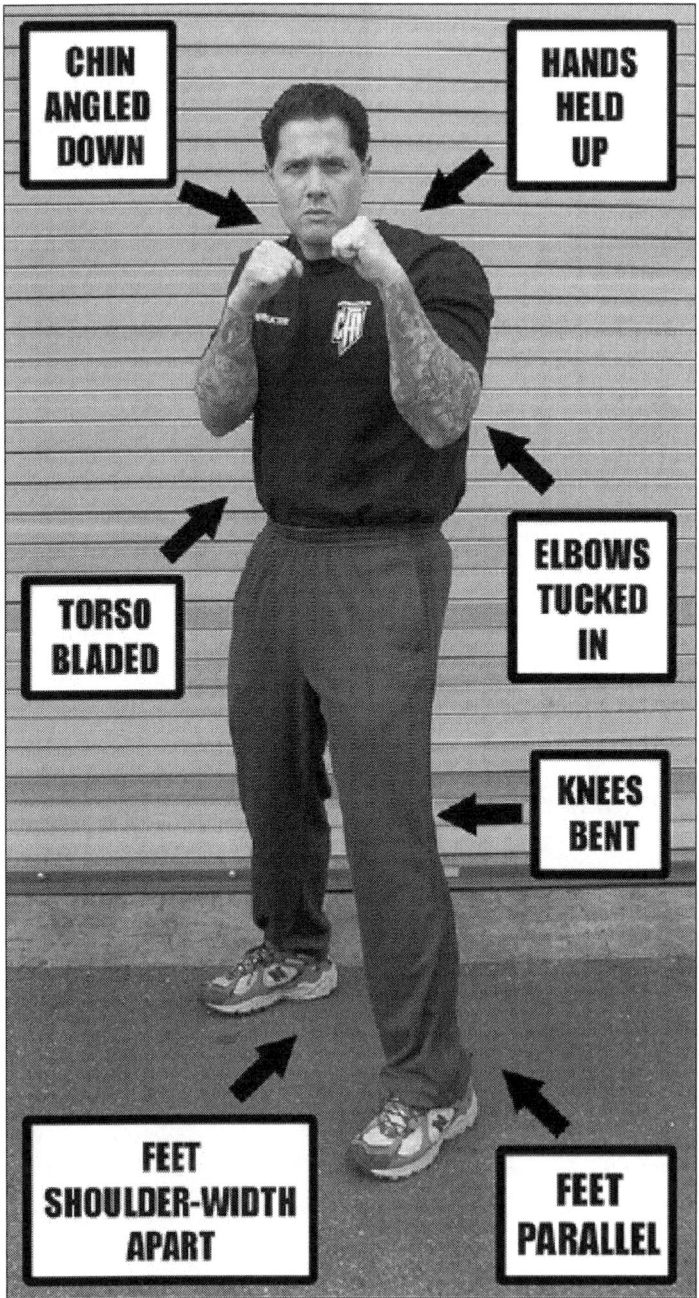

adversary. Unlike the traditional boxer's stance, you don't need to keep your chin pinned down against your collar bone. Such action will lead to premature fatigue and inhibit the speed and delivery of your hand strikes. Just remember to keep your head and chin slightly angled down. This diminishes target size and reduces the likelihood of a paralyzing blow to the chin or a lethal strike to the throat.

The Torso

The centerline of your torso should be strategically positioned at a 45-degree angle from your adversary. When assuming a fighting stance, place your strongest, most coordinated side forward. For example, a right-handed person stands with his or her right side toward the assailant. Keeping your strongest side forward enhances the speed, power, and accuracy of your first strike. This doesn't mean that you should never practice fighting from your other side. You

Left lead fighting stance (lateral view).

Right lead fighting stance (lateral view).

must be capable of fighting from both sides, and you should spend equal practice time on the left and right stances.

The Lead and Rear Arms

The hands are aligned one behind the other along your centerline. The lead arm is held high and bent at approximately 90 degrees. The rear arm is kept back by the chin. Arranged this way, the hands not only protect the torso centerline but also allow quick deployment of your body weapons. When holding your guard, do not tighten your shoulder or arm muscles prior to striking. Stay relaxed and loose.

The Lead and Rear Legs

When assuming your fighting stance, place your feet about shoulder width apart. Keep your knees bent and flexible. Think of your legs as power springs to launch you through the ranges of unarmed self-defense (kicking, punching, and grappling).

Mobility is also important, as we'll discuss later. All footwork and strategic movement should be performed on the balls of your feet. Your weight distribution is also an important factor. Since self-defense is dynamic, your weight distribution will change frequently. However, when stationary, keep 50 percent of your body weight on each leg and always be in control of it.

Many people make the costly mistake of stepping forward to assume a fighting stance. ***Do not do this!*** This action only moves you

When assuming a fighting stance, the distance between your feet is a critical factor. If your feet are too close to each other you will lack the necessary balance to maintain an effective fighting structure. If your feet are too far apart you'll be rigid and static, thus restricting your ability to move quickly. However, by keeping your feet approximately shoulder-width apart, you will provide your stance with sufficient balance and stability without sacrificing mobility.

closer to your assailant before your protective structure is soundly established. Moving closer to your assailant also dramatically reduces your defensive reaction time. So get into the habit of stepping backwards to assume your stance. Practice this daily until it becomes a natural and economical movement.

Psychological Implications of the Fighting Stance

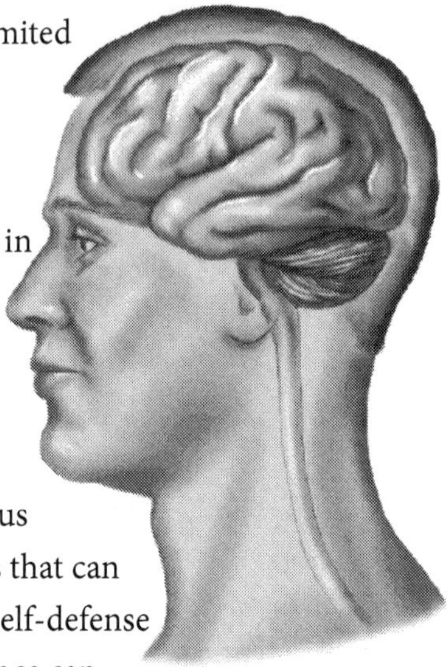

The fighting stance is not just limited to the physical plane of unarmed combat. As a matter of fact, it can directly influence your opponent's behavior and it plays a material role in the psychological aspects of hand-to-hand combat.

You must remember that combat is not just won by physical techniques alone. There are numerous psychological nuances and elements that can make a tremendous difference in a self-defense situation. In some cases, this difference can mean life or death.

From a psychological perspective, a solid fighting stance must project the following positive characteristics to the adversary:

1. **You must appear experienced** - The fighting stance must make you appear like a "seasoned" or veteran fighter. When your opponent observes your stance, he should perceive an experienced fighter who is no stranger to violence.
2. **You must appear skilled** - Your fighting stance should also project a skilled fighter. Remember, just because you appear experienced, doesn't necessarily mean you look skilled.

Street punks, thugs, and barroom brawlers will be able to assess your posture and determine if you really "know what you are doing." In the blink of an eye, they will scan your fighting stance to quickly identify any telltale signs of a novice. Some indicators might include: curling your wrists, wide eyes, overly tight fists, excessive blinking or sweating, centerline exposure, limb shaking, etc.

3. **You must appear aggressive or menacing** - Unlike the other strategic stances featured in this book, the fighting stance is truly devoid of strategic deception. In many ways, it's a threatening and primitive posture that must project raw aggression to the opponent.

A solid fighting stance can also have a positive impact on your own attitude and behavior during the fight. However, this requires that the following requirements are met.

1. **It must feel natural** - Your fighting stance must feel natural to you. It should not feel mechanical or artificial to you. Constant repetition and practice is the only real way to make the stance become one with you.
2. **It must feel comfortable** - Your fighting stance must also feel physically comfortable. When assuming the stance, it must immediately create a psychological "comfort zone." If your stance feels awkward or rigid, then now is the time to modify it so it works for you.
3. **It must feel warlike** - When you assume the stance, it should also make you feel warlike. This is important both consciously and subconsciously. On a conscious level, it will empower you to meet the stressful challenges that face you. It will help instill an immediate positive attitude which is so vital to surviving the dangerous rigors of unarmed fighting.

On a subconscious level, this warlike feeling will help ignite and maintain your killer instinct during the altercation. The killer instinct is a vicious combat mentality that surges to your consciousness and turns you into a fierce fighter who is free of fear, anger, and apprehension. If you want to survive the horrifying dynamics of real criminal violence, you must cultivate and utilize this killer instinct mentality.

Fighting Stance Overview

- Used as reference point for both offensive and defensive techniques or during a sudden pause in combat engagement
- Chin angled down
- Torso centerline positioned at 45 degrees from opponent
- Strongest side of body faces adversary
- Shoulders and arms are relaxed but ready
- Hands are held up and wrists are straight
- Rear arm is kept back close to face
- Elbows point down to the ground
- 50% percent weight distribution on both legs
- Knees are bent, flexible, and ready
- Feet set approximately shoulder width apart

When assuming a fighting stance, align both your rear and lead hands. This will protect your centerline, temporarily negate the assailant's linear assault, and set up your body weapons. Never open your hands and expose your centerline in an attempt to draw your assailant's attack. You'll get hurt! The open-hand guard is only used for the bludgeon- defense stance.

Fighting Stance Drill (Shadow Fighting)

Shadow fighting is one of the best exercises you can do to improve your fighting stance. Essentially, shadow fighting is the creative deployment of offensive and defensive tools and maneuvers against imaginary assailants from the reference point of a fighting stance.

Shadow fighting requires intense mental concentration, honest self-analysis, and a deep commitment to improve. For those of you on a tight budget, the good news is that shadow fighting is inexpensive. All you need is a full-length mirror and a place to work out. The mirror is vital. It functions as a critic, your personal instructor. If you're honest, the mirror will be too. It will point out every mistake

- poor stance structure, telegraphing, sloppy footwork, poor body mechanics, and even lack of physical conditioning.

Proper shadow fighting develops speed, power, balance, footwork, compound attack skills, sound form, and finesse. It even promotes a better understanding of the ranges of combat. As you progress, you can incorporate light dumbbells into shadow fighting workouts to enhance power and speed. Start off with one to three pounds and gradually work your way up. A weight vest can also be worn to develop powerful footwork, kicks, and knee strikes.

If you want to make your fighting stance instinctual, practice it in a slow and controlled fashion with your eyes closed. Closing your eyes when training will help you develop a complete kinesthetic feel for the movement.

When shadow fighting be especially aware of the following:

1. Dropping your hands down when moving around.
2. Punching low.
3. Lifting your chin up.
4. Elbows flaring out to the sides.
5. Tensing your muscles before, during and after technique deployment.
6. Unnecessary widening of your feet.
7. Cross stepping when moving sideways.
8. Failing to maintain a 45-degree angle stance.
9. Excessive weight distribution.
10. Dancing around, showing off or showboating.

Mobility

Next are footwork and mobility. I define mobility as the ability to move your body quickly and freely, which is accomplished through basic footwork. The safest footwork involves quick, economical steps performed on the balls of your feet, while you remain relaxed and balanced. Keep in mind that balance is your most important consideration.

Basic footwork can be used for both offensive and defensive purposes, and it is structured around four general directions: forward, backward, right, and left. However, always remember this footwork rule of thumb: Always move the foot closest to the direction you want to go first, and let the other foot follow an equal distance. This prevents cross-stepping, which can cost you your life in a fight.

Basic Footwork Movements

1. **Moving forward (advance)** - from your fighting stance, first move your front foot forward (approximately 12 inches) and then move your rear foot an equal distance.

2. **Moving backward (retreat)** - from your fighting stance, first move your rear foot backward (approximately 12 inches) and then move your front foot an equal distance.

3. **Moving right (sidestep right)** - from your fighting stance, first move your right foot to the right (approximately 12 inches) and then move your left foot an equal distance.

4. **Moving left (sidestep left)** - from your fighting stance, first move your left foot to the left (approximately 12 inches) and then move your right foot an equal distance.

Practice these four movements for 10 to 15 minutes a day in front of a full-length mirror. In a couple weeks, your footwork should be quick, balanced, and natural.

Circling Right and Left

Strategic circling is an advanced form of footwork where you will use your front leg as a pivot point. This type of movement can also be used defensively to evade an overwhelming assault or to strike the opponent from various strategic angles. Strategic circling can be performed from either a left or right stance.

Circling left (from a left stance) - this means you'll be moving your body around the opponent in a clockwise direction. From a left stance, step 8 to 12 inches to the left with your left foot, then use your left leg as a pivot point and wheel your entire rear leg to the left until the correct stance and positioning is acquired.

Circling right (from a right stance) - from a right stance, step 8 to 12 inches to the right with your right foot, then use your right leg as a pivot point and wheel your entire rear leg to the right until the correct stance and positioning is acquired.

Chapter 4
Sucker Punch Arsenal

Sucker Punch Striking Techniques

In this chapter, I'm going to teach you several devastating sucker punch strikes. Unlike the other offensive tools, these techniques were chosen because they are efficient, effective, and virtually non-telegraphic.

Finger Jab to the Eyes

The finger jab is a quick, non-telegraphic strike executed from your lead arm. Contact is made with your fingertips. To execute the finger jab, quickly shoot your arm out and back. Don't tense your muscles before the execution of the strike. Just relax and send it out. Targets for the finger jab are the assailant's eyes. Don't forget that a finger jab strike can cause temporary or permanent blindness, severe pain, and shock. Remember, with the finger jab, you want speed, accuracy, and, above all, non-telegraphic movement.

Hammer Fist to the Nose

The rear vertical hammer fist (short arc) is a quick and powerful sucker punch that is delivered at close range to the adversary. Your target is the assailant's nose. To deliver the vertical hammer fist, begin by raising your fist with your elbow flexed. Quickly whip your clenched fist down in a vertical line onto the bridge of your assailant's nose. Remember to keep your elbow bent on impact and maintain your balance throughout execution.

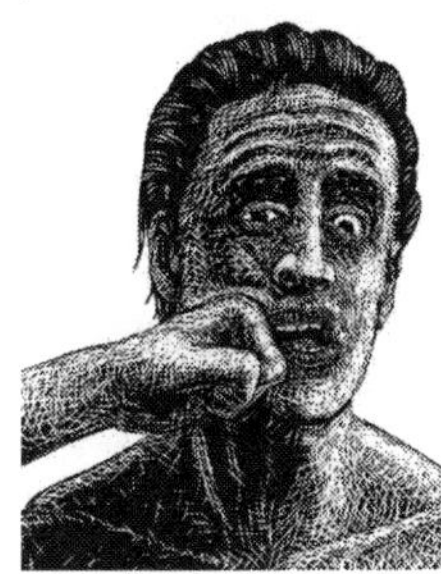

Not all sucker punches are fisted blows, some include open hand strikes.

Palm Strike to the Nose or Chin

The rear palm-heel strike is a powerful open-hand linear blow that is capable of knocking out the toughest opponent. Contact is made with the heel of your palm with the fingers pointing up. Targets include your assailant's nose and chin.

When delivering the blow, be certain to torque your shoulder, hips, and foot in the direction of the strike. Make certain that your arm extends straight out and that the heel of your palm makes contact with either the assailant's nose or chin. Remember to retract your arm along the same line in which you initiated the strike.

Web Hand Strike to the Throat

The web hand strike is a grappling-range sucker punch technique that can produce devastating results. Depending on the amount of force, a strike to the throat can cause gagging, excruciating pain, loss of breath, nausea, and possibly death.

To perform the strike, simultaneously separate your thumb from your index finger and quickly drive the web of your hand into the adversary's throat. Be certain to keep your hand stiff with your palm down. Once contact is made, quickly retract your hand to the starting position. WARNING: The web hand strike should only be used in life-and-death situations! Be certain that it is legally warranted and justified.

Uppercut to the Chin

The rear uppercut is the mother of all punches. When executed properly it can take any man out of a fight. This knockout punch travels in a vertical direction to the adversary's chin or body.

To execute the rear uppercut, quickly twist and lift the rear side of your body into the direction of the blow. Make certain that the blow has a tight arc and that you avoid any telegraphing.

Elbow Strike to the Face

The rear horizontal elbow is a devastating weapon used in grappling range. It is explosive, deceptive, and very difficult to stop. The rear horizontal elbow strike travels horizontally to the assailant's face. Targets can include the nose, temple, and ear.

To perform the strike, quickly rotate your hips and shoulders horizontally into your target. Your palms should be facing downward with your hand next to the side of your head. The striking surface is the elbow point.

Head Butt to the Nose or Chin

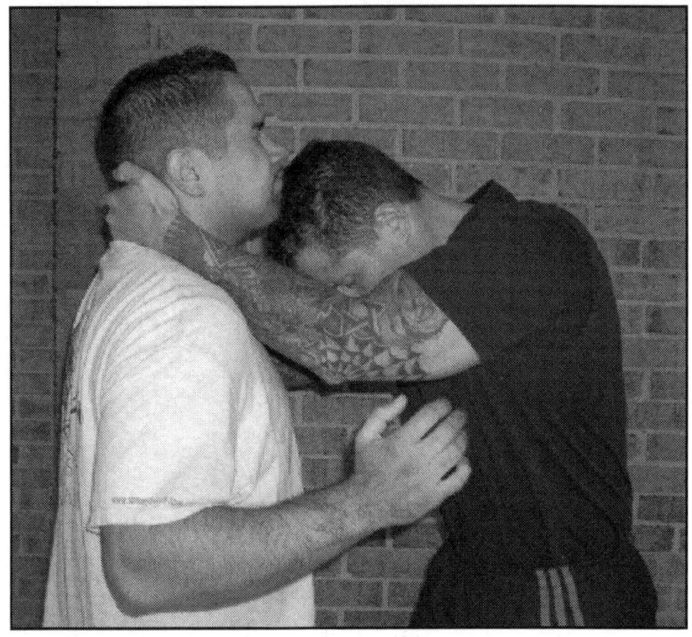

When you are fighting in close quarters, your head can be used for butting your assailant's nose. Head butts are ideal when a strong attacker has placed you in a hold where your arms are pinned against your sides. Keep in mind that the head butt can be delivered in four different directions: forward, backward, right side, and left side.

Have a Backup Plan, Just In Case!

The ultimate goal of a sucker punch is to quickly put an end to a fight with one decisive blow. However, you must have a backup plan and be prepared if your preemptive strike doesn't neutralize the threat. Remember, you cannot afford the risk that one perfectly executed punch, strike, or other technique will terminate the fight.

To drive the point home, think of the now familiar law enforcement stories of drug-induced criminal aggressors who keep coming after being hit by a .40 caliber bullet. There are a lot of those types of people out there, and they're often involved in violent street attacks.

The bottom line is, you cannot rely on a sucker punch to stop such a dangerous assailant. In almost every case you won't know your aggressor's pain tolerance, his state of mind or capability for violence.

However, there's nothing wrong with developing the capability to knock your opponent out with a single blow. In fact, it can be done if you are willing to invest the time and energy to training.

Just remember, it might take more than just a sucker punch to stop your adversary. To complete the job, you might have to initiate a strategic compound attack.

Compound Your Hits

A compound attack is what immediately follows your sucker punch, and it's defined as the logical sequence of two or more tools strategically thrown in succession. The objective is to take the fight out of the assailant and the assailant out of the fight by destroying his defenses with a flurry of full-speed, full-force strikes.

Based on power, accuracy, speed and commitment, the compound attack also requires calculation, control and clarity. In other words, the unskilled, untrained brawler who goes off with a buzzsaw of violent strikes is not executing a compound attack. There is more to it than that.

The compound attack starts with a thorough understanding and knowledge of every conceivable anatomical target presented by the various stances, angles, distances, and movements of the opponent. Unless he is in full body armor, there are always targets. It is a question of recognizing them and striking quickly with the appropriate tools. This requires mastery of a wide range of offensive techniques, a complete understanding of combat ranges, reaction dynamic awareness, and the proper use of force.

But remember, what is universally true for all opponents is equally true for you. If there is always a target available on him, there's always one on you – although vulnerability can be reduced with proper training. Remember, strike first, strike fast, strike with authority, and keep the pressure on.

As you attack one target, others open up naturally. It is up to you to recognize them through reaction dynamic awareness and keep the offensive flow. Executed properly, the compound attack demolishes your opponents defenses that you ultimately take him down and out. It sounds great, but you must realize that it has to happen within seconds.

Secondary Strikes

Now that we have covered the sucker punch arsenal, it's time to take a look at secondary strikes. Essentially, secondary strikes are offensive techniques that are executed in the event your sucker punch doesn't knock out your adversary. For the most part, secondary strikes techniques comprise the bulk of your compound attack arsenal. We'll begin with the hook kick.

The Hook Kick

The hook kick is a circular kick that is thrown from your rear leg. Contact is made with either your instep or shinbone. To execute the hook kick, step at a 45-degree angle and simultaneously twist and drive your rear leg and hip into your assailant's target. Make certain to pivot your base foot and follow through your target. When executing the hook kick, either aim for your assailant's knee or drive your shin into the assailant's common peroneal nerve (approximately four inches above the knee area). This will collapse and temporarily immobilize the assailant's leg. Keep in mind that if you strike the knee you can cause permanent damage to the cartilage, ligaments, tendons, and bones.

Lead Straight

The lead straight is a linear punch thrown from your lead arm, and contact is made with the center knuckle. To execute the lead straight, quickly twist your lead leg, hip, and shoulder forward. Snap your blow into the assailant's target and return to the starting position. A common mistake is to throw the punch and let it deflect to the side. Targets for the lead straight include the nose, chin, and solar plexus.

Rear Cross

The rear cross is the most powerful linear tool in your unarmed arsenal. This punch travels in a straight direction to your assailant's nose, chin, or solar plexus. Proper waist twisting and weight transfer are of paramount importance to the rear cross. You must shift your weight from your rear foot to your lead leg as you throw the punch. You can generate bone-crushing force by torquing your rear foot, hip, and shoulder into the direction of the blow. To maximize the impact of the punch, make certain that your fist is positioned horizontally. Avoid overextending the blow or exposing your chin during its execution.

Lead Hook Punch

The lead hook punch is one of the most difficult to master. To execute the punch properly, you must maintain the correct wrist, forearm, and shoulder alignment. When delivering the strike, be certain that your arm is bent at least 90 degrees and that your wrist and forearm are kept straight throughout the movement.

To execute the punch, quickly and smoothly raise your elbow so that your arm is parallel to the ground while simultaneously torquing your shoulder, hip, and foot into the direction of the blow. As you throw the punch, be certain that your fist is positioned vertically. Never position your fist horizontally when throwing a hook: this inferior hand placement can cause a sprained or broken wrist. Avoid chambering or cocking the blow and excessive follow-through.

Rear Hook Punch

The rear hook punch is one of the most devastating blows in your arsenal. As with the lead hook, it will take considerable time to master. When delivering the rear hook punch, you must maintain correct wrist, forearm, and shoulder alignment. Once again, your arm must be bent at least 90 degrees while your wrist and forearm are kept straight throughout the movement.

To execute the rear hook punch, quickly and smoothly raise your elbow so that your arm is parallel to the ground while simultaneously torquing your rear shoulder, hip, and foot into the direction of the blow. As you throw the punch, be certain that your fist is positioned vertically.

Lead Uppercut

The lead uppercut is a powerful blow that can be delivered in both the punching and grappling ranges. This tool travels in a vertical direction to either the assailant's chin or body, and it is delivered from the lead arm.

To execute the lead uppercut, quickly twist and lift the lead side of your body into the direction of the blow. Make certain that the punch has a short arc and that you avoid any "winding-up" motions.

Rear Uppercut

The rear uppercut is considered both a sucker punch and secondary strike technique. As I mentioned earlier, the rear uppercut is a fierce punch. When executed properly, it can knock out just about anyone. Just like the lead uppercut, it travels in a vertical direction to the adversary's chin or body.

To execute the rear uppercut, quickly twist and lift the rear side of your body into the direction of the blow. Make certain that the blow has a tight arc and that you avoid any telegraphing.

Lead Shovel Hook

The lead shovel hook is another powerful punch that travels diagonally into your assailant. To execute the lead shovel hook properly, dip your lead shoulder and simultaneously twist your lead leg and hip into your assailant's target and then drive your entire body into the assailant. Once again, keep balanced and follow through your selected target.

Rear Shovel Hook

To properly execute the rear shovel hook, quickly dip your rear shoulder and simultaneously twist your rear leg and hip into your assailant's target; then drive your entire body into the assailant. Remember to always keep balanced.

Long Arc Hammer Fist

The long arc hammer fist is delivered vertically to either the assailant's neck or spine. To deliver the rear vertical hammer fist, begin by raising your fist with your elbow flexed. Drive your clenched fist down in a vertical line onto the back of your assailant's neck. Be certain to bend at your hips and knees and follow through your target. Remember to keep your elbow bent on impact and maintain your balance throughout execution.

CAUTION: Never deliver a hammer-fist strike with a straight arm. This will rob you of speed and power and possibly cause a severe elbow strain.

Rear Vertical Knee

The rear vertical-knee strike is another devastating close-quarter grappling-range tool that can bring a formidable assailant to the ground. The knee strike travels vertically to a variety of anatomical targets, including the common peroneal nerve, the quadriceps, the groin, the ribs, and, in some cases, the face. When delivering the strike, be certain to make contact with your patella and not your lower thigh. To guarantee sufficient power, deliver all your knee strikes with your rear leg.

Rear Diagonal Knee

The rear diagonal-knee strike is another one that travels on a diagonal plane to the assailant, much like the hook kick. Targets include the common peroneal nerve, quadriceps, groin, ribs, and face. When delivering the strike, don't forget to follow through your target.

Probable Reaction Dynamics (PRD)

In my book, ***Maximum Damage: Hidden Secrets Behind Brutal Fighting Combinations***, I define probable reaction dynamics as the opponent's anticipated or predicted movements or actions that occur in both armed and unarmed combat. Probable reaction dynamics will always be the result or residual of your initial sucker punch.

The most basic example of probable reaction dynamics can be illustrated by the following scenario. Let's say, you are fighting with your adversary and the opportunity presents itself to forcefully kick him in his groin. When your foot comes in contact with its target, your opponent will exhibit one of several "possible" physical or psychological reactions to your strike. These responses might include:

- The opponent's head and body violently drop forward.
- The opponent grabs or covers his groin region.
- The opponent struggles for breath.
- The opponent momentarily freezes.
- The opponent goes into shock.

Knowledge of your assailant's probable reaction dynamics is vital in both armed and unarmed combat. In fact, you must be mindful of the possible reaction dynamics to every kick, punch, strike, and technique in your arsenal. This is exactly what I refer to as *reaction dynamic awareness* and I can assure you this is not such an easy task. However, with proper training, it can be developed.

Regardless of your style of fighting, understanding and ultimately mastering reaction dynamic awareness will give you a tremendous advantage in a fight by maximizing the effectiveness, efficiency and safety of your compound attack.

Flow like Water!

When you proceed with the compound attack, always maintain the offensive flow. The offensive flow is a progression of continuous offensive movements designed to neutralize your opponent. The key is to have each strike flow smoothly and efficiently from one to the next without causing you to lose ground. Subjecting your adversary to an offensive flow is especially effective because it taxes his nervous system, thereby dramatically lengthening his defensive reaction time.

In a real-life street fight it's critical that you always keep the offensive pressure on until your opponent is completely neutralized. Always remember that letting your offensive flow stagnate, even for a second, will open you up to numerous dangers and risks.

Proper breathing is another substantial element of the compound attack, and there is one simple rule that should be followed: exhale during the execution phase of your strike and inhale during its retraction phase. Above all, never hold your breath when delivering several consecutive blows. Doing so could lead to dizziness and fainting, among other complications.

Time is a Factor!

Your body can only sustain delivering a compound attack for so long. Initially, your brain will quickly release adrenaline or epinephrine into your blood stream, which will fuel your fighting and enhance your strength and power. This lethal boost of energy is known as an adrenaline dump. However, your ability to exert and maintain this maximum effort in a compound attack will last no more than 30 to 60 seconds if you are in above-average shape. If the fight continues after that, your strength and speed may drop by as much as 50 percent below normal. When all is said and done, you don't have much time in a fight, so the battle needs to be won fast before your energy runs out!

Don't Forget to Relocate

Subsequent to your compound attack, immediately move to a new location by flanking your adversary. This tactic is known as relocating. The best way to accomplish this is through circling footwork. Based on the principles of strategy, movement, and surprise, relocating dramatically enhances your safety by making it difficult for your adversary to identify your position after you have attacked him. Remember, if your opponent doesn't know exactly where you are, he won't be able to effectively counterattack.

Combat Attributes

A sucker punch or any fighting technique for that matter is useless unless it is accompanied by certain combative attributes. Attributes are qualities that enhance your sucker punch technique.

For example, speed, power, timing, non telegraphic movement, rhythm, coordination, accuracy, balance, and range specificity are just a few self-defense attributes that must be present if a sucker punch is to be effective in a high-risk self-defense situation.

Let's explore a few basic attributes necessary for fighting: speed, power, timing, balance, and non telegraphic movement.

Speed

To effectively land any offensive strike you must possess speed. By speed, I am referring to how fast your body weapon moves to its target. A fast technique should be likened to the strike of a snake. It should be felt and not seen by your assailant.

While some athletes are blessed with great speed, you should make every possible attempt to develop your speed to the maximum of your ability. One of the easiest ways of enhancing your speed is to simply relax your body prior to executing your body weapon. For example, when executing a palm heel strike to your assailant's chin, your arm should simply shoot straight out and back to its starting point without muscular tension. This may sound simple, but you'd be amazed how many people have difficulty relaxing—especially when they are under tremendous stress. Another way of developing blinding speed is to practice throwing all of your offensive weapons in the air. Focus on quickly executing and retracting your tool or technique as quickly as you can. If you are persistent and work diligently, you can achieve significant results.

Power

Power refers to the amount of impact force you can generate when striking your target. The power of your sucker punch is not necessarily predicated on your size and strength. A relatively small person can generate devastating power if he or she combines it with sufficient speed. This explains why someone like Bruce Lee who weighed approximately 130 pounds could hit harder than most 200-pound men. Lee knew how to maximize his impact power through the speed at which he executed his techniques.

Ideally, when attempting to strike your assailant, you want to put your entire body behind your blow. I instruct my students to always aim 3 inches through their chosen target. Torquing your hips and shoulder into your blows will also help generate tremendous power. Remember, in a real self-defense situation, you want to hit your assailant with the power equivalent of a shotgun and not a squirt gun.

Timing

Timing refers to your ability to execute a sucker punch at the optimum moment. There are two types of timing: defensive and offensive. Defensive timing is the time between the assailant's attack and your defensive response to that attack. Offensive timing is the time between your recognition of a target opening and your offensive response to that opening.

Among the best ways of developing both offensive and defensive timing are stick and knife fighting, sparring sessions, double-end bag training, and various focus mitt drills. Mental visualization is also another effective method of enhancing timing. Visualizing various self-defense scenarios that require precise timing is ideal for enhancing your skills.

Balance

Effectively striking your assailant requires substantial follow-through while maintaining your balance. Balance is your ability to maintain equilibrium while stationary or moving. You can maintain perfect balance only through controlling your center of gravity, mastering body mechanics, and proper skeletal alignment.

To develop your sense of balance, perform your sucker punch techniques slowly so you become acquainted with the different weight distributions, body positions, and mechanics of each particular weapon. For example, when executing an elbow strike, keep your head, torso, legs, and feet in proper relation to each other. Be certain to follow through your target, but don't overextend yourself.

Non Telegraphic Movement

The element of surprise is an invaluable tool for self-defense. Successfully landing a sucker punch requires that you do not forewarn your assailant of your intentions. Clenching your teeth, widening your eyes, cocking your fist, and tensing your neck or shoulders are just a few common telegraphic cues that will negate the element of surprise.

One of the best ways to prevent telegraphic movement is to maintain a poker face prior to executing your body weapon or technique. Avoid all facial expressions when faced with a threatening assailant. As mentioned, you can study your techniques and maneuvers in front of a full-length mirror or have a friend videotape you performing your movements. These procedures will assist you in identifying and ultimately eliminating telegraphic movements. Be patient and you'll reach your objective.

Chapter 5
Sucker Punch Targets

Targets that Count!

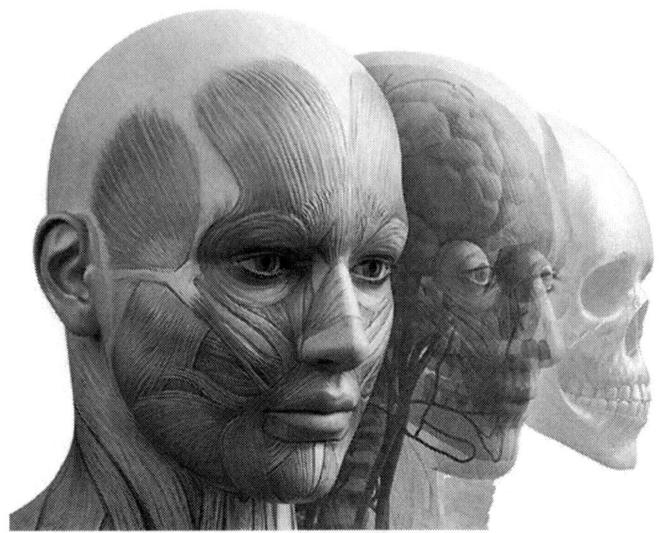

Now that you're familiar with both sucker punch and secondary strike techniques, it's time to learn about targeting. Remember, knowing how and when to sucker punch your opponent is essential; however knowing *where* to hit him is equally important. Therefore, anyone who is seriously interested in neutralizing a formidable assailant must have a working knowledge and understanding of the targets on the human anatomy.

Many people don't realize that the human body has many structural weaknesses that are especially vulnerable to attack. The human body simply was not designed to take the punishment of strikes and blows. Always keep in mind that regardless of your attacker's size, strength, or state of mind, he or she will always have vulnerable targets that can be attacked. Sucker punch targets are divided into two unique categories, they are:

- **Primary targets**
- **Follow-up targets**

Primary Targets

Primary sucker punch targets are specific anatomical areas that are particularly vulnerable to a preemptive strike. Unlike other anatomical targets, these are especially weak and vulnerable to attack. More importantly, all of these targets can be found on the opponent's face and head. They include the following:

- **Eyes**
- **Temple**
- **Nose**
- **Chin**
- **Throat**

Let's begin by looking at each target. We will start with the opponent's eyes.

EYES

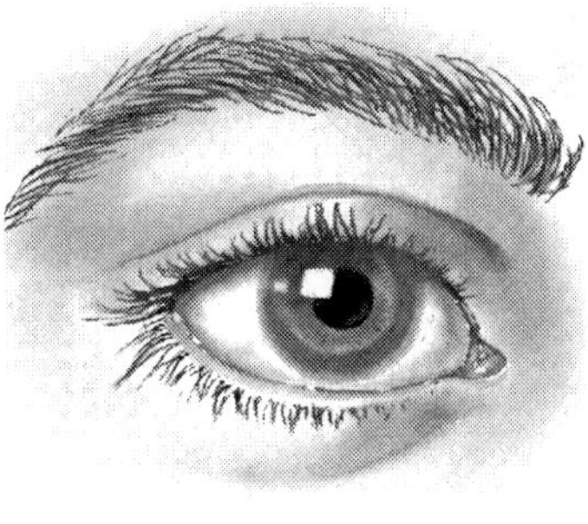

Eyes sit in the orbital bones of the skull. They are ideal targets for a sucker punch because they are extremely sensitive and difficult to protect, and striking them requires very little force. The eyes can be poked, scratched, and gouged from a variety of angles. Depending on the force of your strike, it can cause numerous injuries, including watering of the eyes, hemorrhaging, blurred vision, temporary or permanent blindness, severe pain, rupture, shock, and unconsciousness.

NOSE

The nose is made up of a thin bone, cartilage, numerous blood vessels, and many nerves. It is a particularly good sucker punch target because it stands out from the opponent's face and can be struck from three different directions (up, straight, down). A moderate blow can cause stunning pain, eye-watering, temporary blindness, and hemorrhaging. A powerful strike can result in shock and unconsciousness.

CHIN

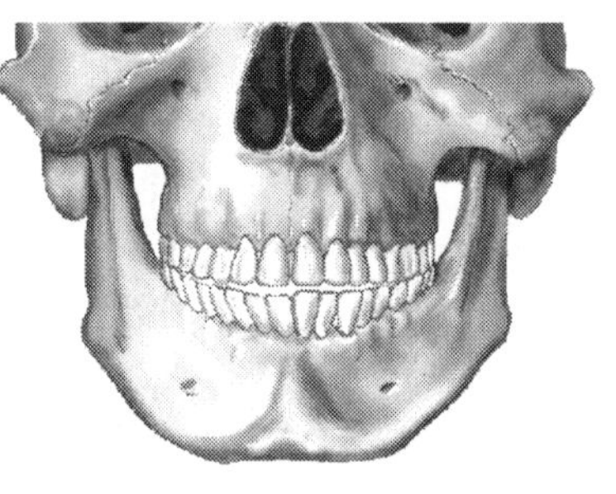

In boxing, the chin is considered a "knockout button," responsible for retiring hundreds of boxers. The chin is equally a good target for sucker punching. When it is struck at a 45-degree angle, shock is transmitted to the cerebellum and cerebral hemispheres of the brain, resulting in paralysis and immediate unconsciousness. Other possible injuries include broken jaw, concussion, and whiplash to the neck.

Target orientation means having a workable knowledge of the various anatomical targets presented before and after you deliver a sucker punch.

TEMPLE

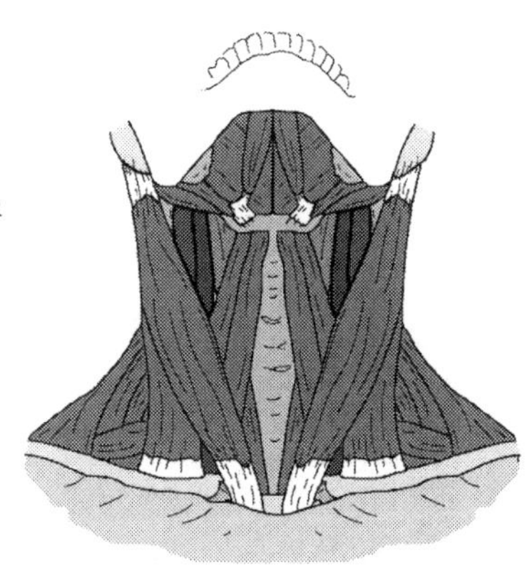

The temple or sphenoid bone is a thin, weak bone located on the side of the skull approximately 1 inch from the eyes. Because of its fragile structure and close proximity to the brain, a powerful strike to this target can be deadly. Other injuries include unconsciousness, hemorrhage, concussion, shock, and coma.

THROAT

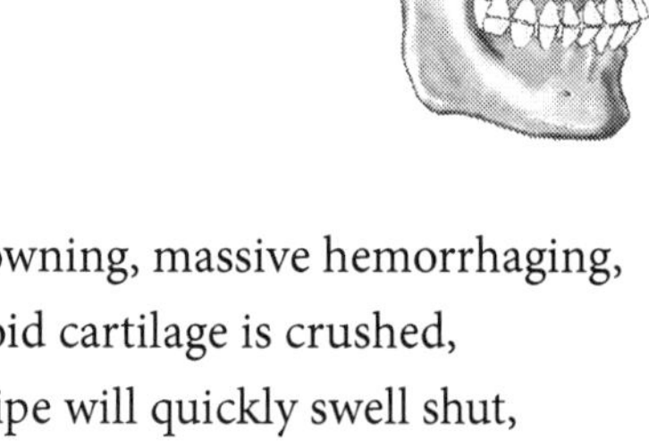

The throat is a lethal sucker punch target because it is only protected by a thin layer of skin. This region consists of the thyroid, hyaline and crocoid cartilage, trachea, and larynx. The trachea, or windpipe, is a cartilaginous tube that measures 4 1/2 inches in length and is approximately 1 inch in diameter. A powerful strike to this target can result in unconsciousness, blood drowning, massive hemorrhaging, air starvation, and death. If the thyroid cartilage is crushed, hemorrhaging will occur, the windpipe will quickly swell shut, resulting in suffocation.

Follow-Up Targets

Follow-up sucker punch targets are used in the event that you are required to "follow-up" with a second or third offensive strike. For example, in the event your first strike fails to stop your adversary from committing further acts of aggression. Follow-up targets include the following:

- **Back of Neck**
- **Solar Plexus**
- **Ribs**
- **Groin**
- **Throat**
- **Thighs**
- **Knees**
- **Shins**
- **Fingers**
- **Toes/Instep**

BACK OF NECK

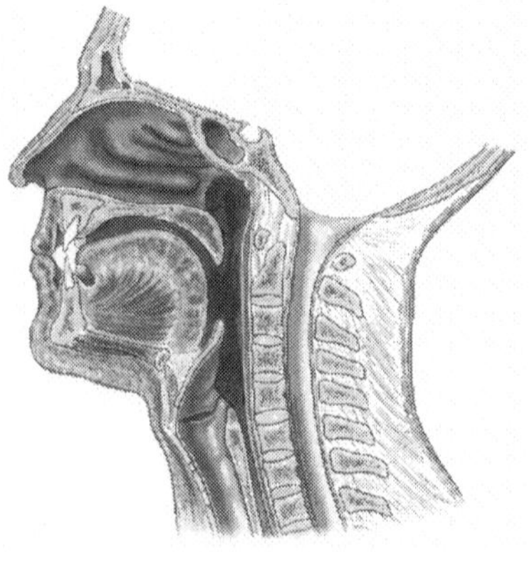

The back of the neck consists of the first seven vertebrae of the spinal column. They act as a circuit board for nerve impulses from the brain to the body. The back of the neck is a lethal target because the vertebrae are poorly protected. A very powerful strike to the back of the neck can cause shock, unconsciousness, a broken neck, complete paralysis, coma, and death.

SOLAR PLEXUS

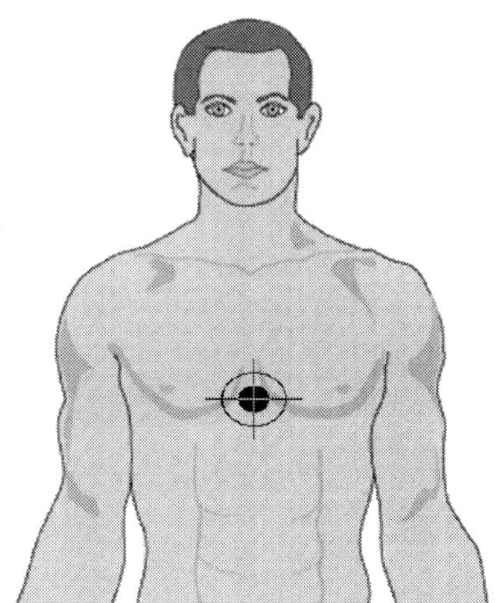

The solar plexus is a large collection of nerves situated below the sternum in the upper abdomen. A moderate blow to this area will cause nausea, tremendous pain, and shock, making it difficult for the assailant to breathe. A powerful strike to the solar plexus can result in severe abdominal pain and cramping, air starvation, and shock.

RIBS

There are 12 pair of ribs in the human body. Excluding the eleventh and twelfth ribs, they are long and slender bones that are joined by the vertebral column in the back and the sternum and costal cartilage in the front.

Since there are no eleventh and twelfth ribs (floating ribs) in the front, you should direct your strikes to the ninth and tenth ribs. A moderate strike to the anterior region of the ribs will cause severe pain and shortness of breath. A powerful 45-degree blow could easily break a rib and force it into a lung, resulting in its collapse, internal hemorrhaging, severe pain, air starvation, unconsciousness, and possible death.

GROIN

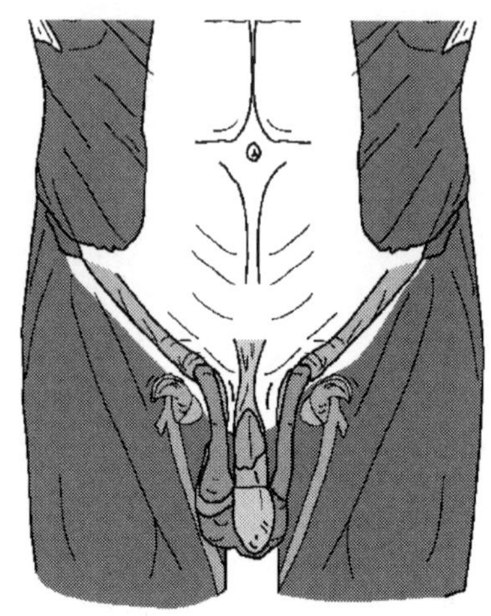

Everyone man will agree that the genitals are highly sensitive organs. Even a light strike can be debilitating. A moderate strike to the groin can result in severe pain, nausea, vomiting, shortness of breath, and possible sterility. A powerful blow to the groin can crush the scrotum and testes against the pubic bones, causing shock and unconsciousness.

THIGHS

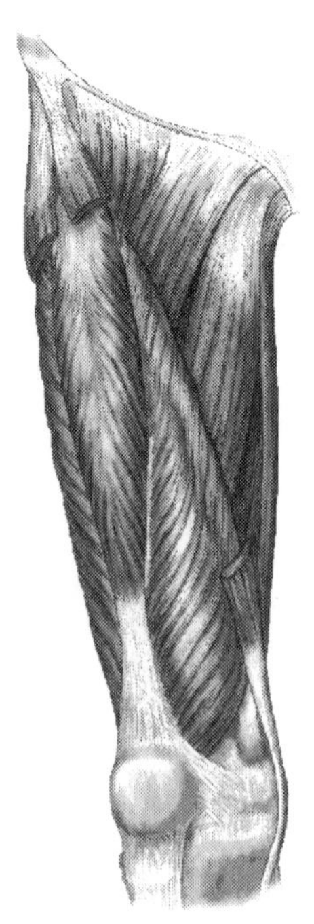

Many people don't realize that the thighs are also vulnerable targets. A moderate kick to the rectus femoris or vastus lateralis muscles will result in immediate immobility of the leg. An extremely hard kick to the thigh can result in a fracture of the femur, resulting in internal bleeding, severe pain, cramping, and immobility of the broken leg.

KNEES

The knee connects the femur to the tibia. It is a very weak joint held together by a number of supporting ligaments. When the assailant's leg is locked or fixed and a forceful strike is delivered to the front of the joint, the cruciate ligaments will tear, resulting in excruciating pain, swelling, and immobility.

Located on the front of the knee joint is the patella, which is made of a small, loose piece of bone. The patella is also extremely vulnerable to dislocation by a direct, forceful kick. Severe pain, swelling, and immobility will quickly result.

SHINS

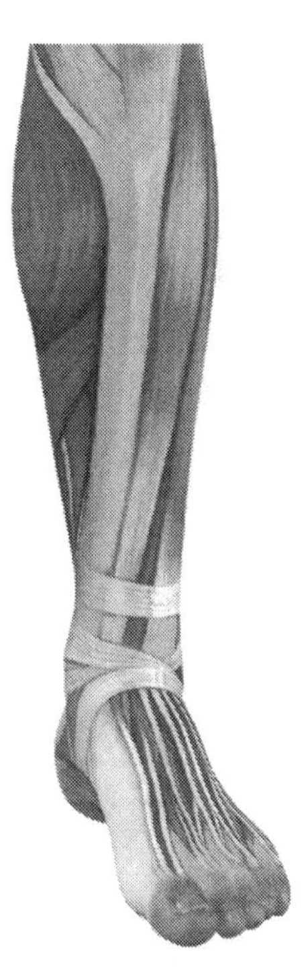

Everyone, at one time or another, has knocked his or her shin bone into the end of a table or bed accidentally and felt the intense pain associated with it. The shin is very sensitive because the bone is only protected by a thin layer of skin. However, a powerful kick delivered to this target can easily fracture it, resulting in nauseating pain, hemorrhaging, and immobility.

FINGERS

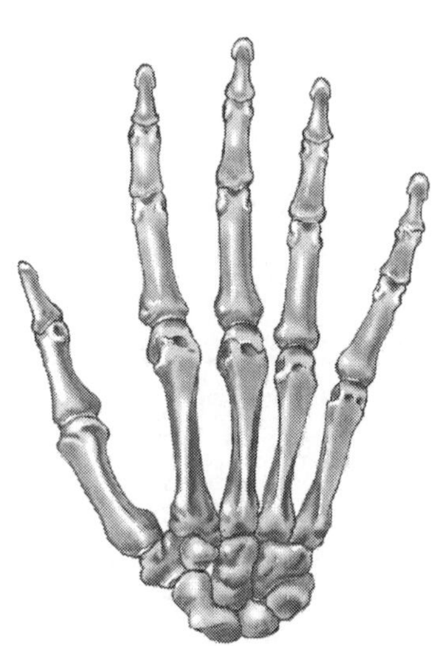

The fingers or digits are considered weak and vulnerable targets that can easily be jammed, sprained, broken, torn, and bitten. While a broken finger might not stop an attacker, it will certainly make him release his hold. A broken finger also makes it difficult for the assailant to clench his fist or hold a weapon. When attempting to break an assailant's finger, it's best to grab the pinkie and forcefully tear backward against the knuckle.

TOES/INSTEP

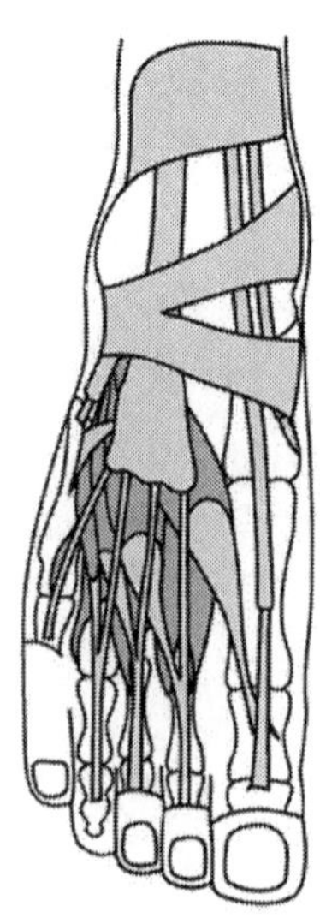

With a powerful stomp of your heel, you can break the small bones of an assailant's toes and or instep, causing severe pain and immobility. Stomping on the toes is an excellent technique for releasing many holds. It should be mentioned, however, that you should avoid an attack to the toes/instep if the attacker is wearing hard leather boots, i.e., combat, hiking, or motorcycle boots.

What follows is a list of ineffective anatomical targets that yield poor results when struck in a street fight. NOTE: This list does not apply to firearms, stick, or knife combat.

- **Coronal Suture (the two frontal and parietal bones)**
- **Mastoid**
- **Sternocleidomastoid region**
- **Brachial Plexus**
- **Trapezius muscle**
- **Clavical (collar bone)**
- **Spleen**
- **Kidneys**
- **Bladder**
- **Biceps**
- **Elbow**
- **Radial nerve**
- **Heart**
- **Abdominal muscles**
- **Coccyx**
- **Gastrocnemius muscle**
- **Achilles tendon**

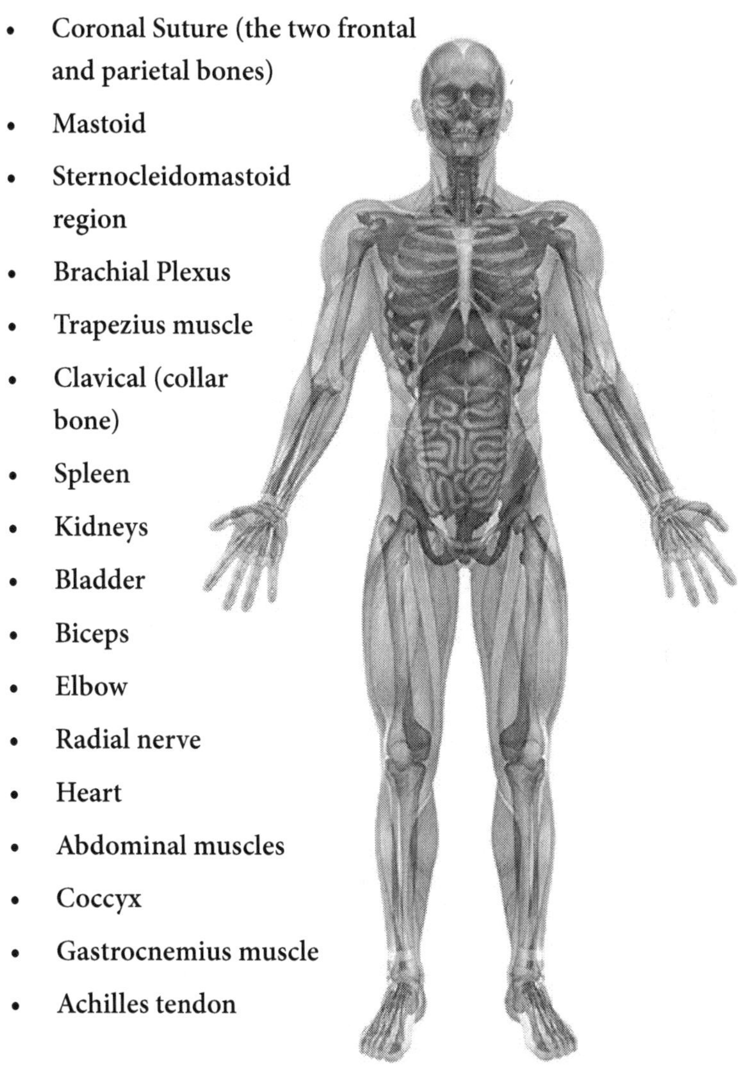

Chapter 6
Sucker Punch Tricks & Techniques

The Art of Trickery and Deception

In this chapter, I'm going to teach you the final component of the set-up - ***sucker punch ruses***. The objective of a sucker punch ruse is to distract and confuse the opponent, whereby lowering his guard and allowing you the opportunity to deliver a devastating first strike. Keep in mind, these unorthodox tricks and deceptions are effective and will work against the most seasoned adversary.

The Sucker Punch Tricks

What follows are some of the best sucker punch techniques. Keep in mind that every self-defense situation will be different and not every tactical ruse is going to be ideal for your particular circumstance. It's up to you to decide which one best suits your needs. Remember to use your best judgment.

Pretend to be a Wimp

This technique is useful when threatened by a larger and stronger adversary. Since large men are accustomed to dominating others through intimidation, this deceptive ruse works like a charm.

Pretend to be a wimp requires some acting on your part. In order to pull it off, you'll need to feign weakness and intimidation to your opponent. The objective is to act like a wimp and make him think you are frightened of him.

For example, when the adversary encroaches on your personal space and threatens you, become apologetic, almost obsequious. Phrases like, "I'm so sorry, please don't hurt me" and "Jesus! I don't want to fight you, you'll kick my ass" seems to work best.

Remember, you are looking to manipulate his ego and gain the tactical advantage, so keep your hands up at all times when pleading with the jerk.

Once the opponent has lowered his guard, and you are in striking range, attack him with one of the sucker punches in your arsenal.

The Coughing Fit

This sucker punch trick is perfect for setting up a surprising first strike. The coughing fit requires you to start coughing during the pre-contact stages of the threat. Initially, your cough should be light and intermittent and build in intensity. Depending on your acting skills, you can also pretend your coughing fit is symptomatic of a stroke or heart attack. Just don't get too carried away! Be convincing, not dramatic!

Since it's proper etiquette to cover your mouth when coughing, you will do so, despite the fact that you are confronted with a hostile adversary. The important part is *how you cover your mouth*. You must remember to bring your hand up to your mouth using a semi-closed fist. This semi-closed fist is a natural and universal accepted gesture that sets up your sucker punch, such as a short arc hammer fist to the opponent's nose.

Once the opponent has lowered his guard, attack him a short art hammer fist blow to his nose.

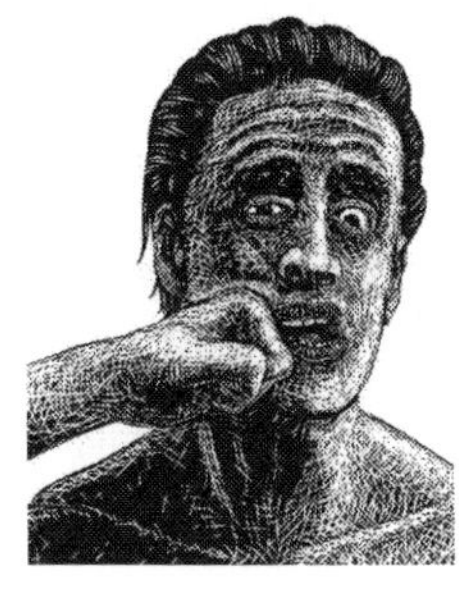

If you feel awkward performing any of the tricks described in this chapter, you might consider first practicing them in front of a mirror or have a training partner videotape your movements. These training procedures are great for evaluating your performance.

The Splash

The *Splash* technique is useful when one or both of your hands are preoccupied holding a drink. The objective of this trick is to temporarily blind your opponent by splashing your drink in his face, giving you free rein to strike.

While almost any liquid will work (i.e., beer, soft drink, water, coffee, etc.), hot liquids tend to work best. However, be mindful that scalding liquids can burn and disfigure the opponent's face, so be certain your actions are justified in the eyes of the law.

The important point is not to telegraph your intentions. Hold your drink at face level while talking and gesticulating with the adversary. Remember to make the drink a natural part of your communication skills before splashing it into his face. Deception is the key.

Over the Shoulder

It was William Shakespeare who said, "The eyes are the window to the soul." But, when it comes to the dirty science of sucker punching, the eyes are windows of deception. Which brings us to my next sucker punch technique called ***Over the Shoulder***.

The Over the Shoulder trick is an effective technique that I have used on a few occasions during my days as a bouncer. The goal is to engage the opponent in conversation, get his attention by looking directly into his eyes, and then glancing over his shoulder to convince him there's a threat behind him. Again, the key is to be subtle, yet convincing.

To effectively execute this trick, perform the following important steps:

1. You must look into the opponent's eyes when communicating with him.
2. Once you make eye contact with the adversary, abruptly stop the conversation (preferably in mid-sentence) and look over his shoulder with a *subtle* look of alarm or concern. You can also point with your finger or use a similar gesture to get the opponent's to look away.
3. The instant your opponent takes the bait and looks over his shoulder, launch your attack.

If you read some of my other books, you'll know that I have regularly stated that you should avoid direct and steady eye contact with the adversary before and during a fight. However, in the case of employing the Over the Shoulder technique, it's permitted.

Spit it Out

Here's a simple and effective trick that exploits your opponent's involuntary reflex response, allowing you to take full advantage of his lapse in attention. However, this technique requires you to have something in your mouth at the time of your altercation. Items like gum, chewing tobacco, and sucking candies tend to work best.

Again, the goal is to make the item in your mouth a natural part of your communication before spitting it at his face. For example, while attempting to diffuse the situation, keep your hands up and ready to attack. Next, spit the item directly into the opponent's face. The second he closes his eyes or looks away, knock him out!

Flick it

This one is similar to the previous trick except you're going to use either a cigarette or a cigar to set-up your sucker punch. Like the Spit it Out technique, you'll want to exploit your opponent's reflex response, allowing you to take full advantage of his lapse in attention.

The important part is to keep your cigarette or cigar in your hands (preferably between your thumb and middle finger) while you are gesticulating and diffusing the situation.

Next, at the ideal moment, flick the cigarette or cigar into the opponent's face, hot embers and all. The second he shuts his eyes or flinches, launch your sucker punch.

Cigarettes, cigars, tobacco pipes, and e-cigarettes can also be used for both the Spit it Out and Flick It trick.

Blow it

This sucker punch technique also requires a cigarette, cigar, tobacco pipe, or e-cigarette to set-up your sucker punch. Like the previous techniques, the goal is to exploit your opponent's involuntary response.

Blow it requires you to literally blow smoke into your opponent's face before launching your sucker punch. The smoke serves as both a distraction and visual impairment. Just be certain the item you are smoking can generate a significant amount of smoke with one exhale. And who said smoke and mirrors don't work in a fight.

Migraine from Hell

A person with a modicum of acting can pull this one off with no problem. The ***Migraine from Hell*** trick requires you to pretend you are suffering from a crippling headache before sucker punching the opponent.

For example, during your confrontation with the opponent, perform the following actions in one fluid gesture. Place your palms on your temples, squint your eyes, and grimace in pain while lowering your body (bending at the knees). Avoid looking at the ground and always keep your eyes fixed on your adversary.

Besides taking the opponent of his guard, this movement sets you up for delivering a knockout uppercut blow to his chin or solar plexus.

The hand gestures used in the Migraine from Hell technique is ideal because it places both of your hands in the perfect spot to launch a non-telegraphic sucker punch.

Scorch Him!

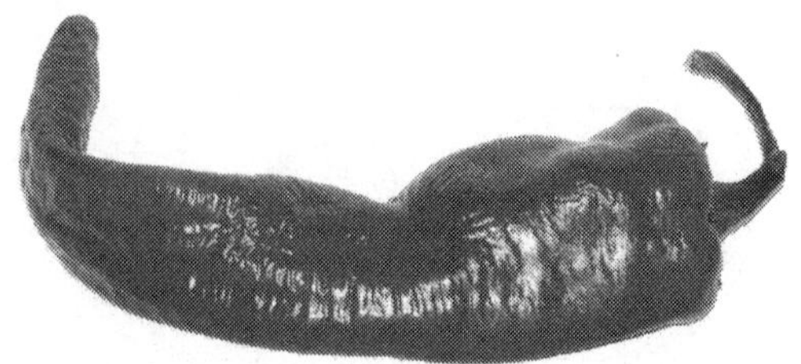

This trick comes straight out of my book, ***Feral Fighting: Advanced Widow Maker Fighting Techniques.*** Scorching is the process of inconspicuously applying oleoresin capsicum (a hot pepper extract) to your fingers tips and then finger jabbing or raking the opponent's eyes.

Scorching is a devastating self-defense tactic that is, by far, the most excruciating form of hand-to-hand combat. It's particularly useful to people who frequent dangerous, high-risk environments and who want to amplify their self-defense skills.

Oleoresin capsicum (also known as OC) is a natural mixture of oil and cayenne pepper. Oleoresin capsicum is found in OC self-defense spray or *pepper spray* and it's an inflammatory agent that affects the assailant's mucus membranes (i.e., eyes, nose, throat, and lungs). When oleoresin capsicum is applied to the mucus membranes, the following reactions will occur:

When you really think about it, the eye rake is a fantastic stand-alone sucker punch technique. Scorching should be viewed as a bonus weapon that amplifies your technique.

- **Eyes will tear and swell shut**
- **Impaired motor skill function**
- **Impaired muscle coordination**
- **Severe burning sensation**
- **Impaired vision for approximately ten minutes**
- **Restricted breathing for about thirty minutes**

Do not use an aerosol pepper spray canister to apply oleoresin capsicum to your fingertips. This is hazardous because you will most likely contaminate yourself and it significantly reduces the potency of OC. Effective scorching will require you to find oleoresin capsicum in a liquid form that can be directly applied to your fingers. There are several on-line manufacturers that sell oleoresin capsicum in liquid form.

There are a couple of ways of applying liquid oleoresin capsicum to your fingertips. One of the best methods is to use my ink pad method, which is inexpensive and just requires you to purchase a dry ink pad from a local office supply store.

Simply pour a liberal amount of liquid OC on the dry pad. To prevent the oleoresin capsicum from evaporating, keep the lid closed at all times and only open it when you must apply it to your fingertips. It's also a good idea to regularly check the ink pad to see if OC residue still remains on the pad.

Warning! Never practice scorching tactics on a live training partner. Serious injury can occur.

Just like self-defense sprays, the OC ink pad can easily be transported in your purse, backpack, briefcase, jacket pocket, car, etc.

A word of caution! *It's your responsibility to check with your local police department regarding the possession and transportation of liquid oleoresin capsicum.*

Over the years, I've conducted hundreds of simulated test scenarios with my students and have determined that you can load liquid oleoresin capsicum on your fingers in less than three seconds. These tests were conducted using my ink pad method of carry. However, a three-second load time requires proper training and practice, and much will also depend on how you carry your liquid OC.

Here, the author demonstrates the ink pad method of application.

Just like carrying a concealed firearm, tactical folder, kubotan, or pepper spray canister, scorching requires you to anticipate danger so you can "prepare and load" the liquid oleoresin capsicum on your fingers before the altercation takes place.

Obviously, if you are ambushed or attacked by surprise, you won't have the time apply the OC and therefore won't be able to scorch you adversary.

When setting up for your scorching attack, remember to keep both of your hands up and away from your face. Once the opponent has lowered his guard, and you're in striking range, attack him with a lightning quick finger jab or eye rake.

Take it Outside

Take it Outside comes in handy when the opponent continues to escalate a dispute, despite your best efforts to diffuse the situation. In simple terms, the jerk just won't let you off the hook.

Take it Outside is best used in crowded environments (i.e., bar, nightclub, restaurant, party, etc.) and formal events where brawling is strictly taboo (i.e., wedding, funeral, family gathering, etc). For example, it's not uncommon for bouncers or security staff to instruct two disputing patrons to settle their differences outside of their establishment.

Timing and positioning are crucial when executing Take it Outside. You should sucker punch the adversary the instant he turns his back and heads for the door. So make certain you're familiar with both lateral and rear sucker punch targets. If necessary, you might need to take another look at Chapter 5 to refresh your memory.

Just a quick reminder: Never deliver a sucker punch unless it's legally warranted and justified in the eyes of the law.

Finally, ***under no circumstances should you turn your back to the enemy and head to the exit first.*** If you are closest to the exit, perform some action or movement that delays your exit and forces the opponent to turn for the door first.

The Lateral Transfer

It's an unfortunate fact of life that sometimes we are forced to sit next to an obnoxious or hostile person. This is especially true for individuals who attend sport or entertainment venues or use public transportation.

The ***Lateral Transfer*** is the ideal tactic when you're sitting side by side with a threatening jerk and your only option is to knock him out. For example, imagine you're sitting next to an unruly troublemaker on a bus, and he's picked you as his next victim. In this circumstance, the Lateral Transfer allows you to inconspicuously knock him out mere seconds before he initiates his attack.

Because of limited space and the awkward angle of the target, your best option is to attack with a horizontal elbow strike delivered from your closest arm. This sucker punch is unexpected because it travels sideways and away from your centerline.

The Lateral Transfer is a great tactic because most people never expect a sucker punch from a seated position.

Catch and Release

Here's another great trick that exploits your opponent's involuntary reflex response, allowing you to take full advantage of him. ***Catch and Release*** is a makeshift weapon tactic that works in tandem with your sucker punch. As I mentioned in a previous chapter, makeshift weapons are common, everyday objects you convert into either offensive or defensive weapons.

For our purposes, we are going to focus on *distracting* makeshift weapons that can be thrown into your assailant's face or upper torso to divert his attention. Distracting makeshift weapons offer some strategic advantages in a fight. Here are just a few:

1. **Element of Surprise** - you can catch the assailant off guard and launch the rest of your offensive attack.
2. **Visual Impairment** - certain objects can temporarily or permanently impair the assailant's vision.
3. **Window of Opportunity** - throwing objects into the assailant's face almost always causes a reaction dynamic that permits you to exploit his sucker punch targets.
4. **Creates a Defensive Flow** - distracting makeshift weapons often force the assailant into a defensive flow.

Some distracting makeshift weapons include: backpacks, briefcases, suitcases, large books, grocery bags, small shipping boxes, loaded cafeteria trays, full face motorcycle helmets, etc.

When using distracting makeshift weapons, be certain the item has the size, weight and structural integrity to get the job done.

The objective of Catch and Release is to throw the item into the opponent's face, forcing him to catch it with both of his hands. The instance he's off his guard, attack him with a punishing attack.

Step 1: Franco (right) is threatened by the opponent.

Step 2: He throws the briefcase at his opponent's face.

Step 3: Franco exploits his opponent's reflex response and attacks with a hook kick. NOTE: Since the briefcase obstructs a direct hit to the head, Franco's uses a low-line kick instead.

Step 4: He follows up with a powerful rear hook punch.

Fifth-Column Tactic

Sucker punching is not just limited to *your* personal safety. It's also useful when a significant other (e.g., close friend, spouse, acquaintance, co-worker, partner) needs help. I call this the ***Fifth-Column Tactic*** and it requires you to follow six important steps:

1. When the hostile and threatening adversary confronts your friend, you should manipulate and soften him up by taking his side in the argument, regardless of how ridiculous his position might be.
2. Always appear nonthreatening and yielding to the adversary by assuming a unaggressive stance or posture.
3. Speak to the adversary in a calm, unresisting tone of voice and be certain to tell him that you and your friend have no intentions of fighting.
4. Next, distract and confuse the opponent by becoming angry with your friend. Raise your voice and castigate your friend for quarreling with the adversary (this will require a good bit of acting on your part).
5. While sympathizing with the opponent, reposition yourself to the most advantageous striking position.
6. Once you have attained the ideal striking position and your partner is out of the line of fire, sucker punch the adversary and keep the pressure on until he is thoroughly incapacitated.

If you ever plan on using the Fifth-Column Tactic, it's best to first practice with you spouse, drinking buddy, wingman, etc. so they will know what to expect.

Fist Loading

Fist Loading is a nasty sucker punch trick that will send your opponent straight to the hospital emergency room. Fist loading is the process of delivering a fisted blow with a concealed object held in your hand. The fist loading object has two important requirements:

1. **Weight** - If you want to pack a wallop, the object must have a minimum weight of seven ounces. It's this slight, extra weight that amplifies the power of your sucker punch.
2. **Structural Integrity** - The object must be solid in construction and provide the structural integrity to reinforce your fist and prevent it from collapsing during impact.

Some practical and effective fist loading objects include metal kubotans, yawaras, tactical flashlights, and rolled coins (quarters or nickels are preferred).

I'd be remiss if I didn't mention that brass knuckles are one of the best fist loading tools known to man. Unfortunately, they are illegal, and therefore, should not be used in a fight.

Other Sucker Punch Fist Loading Tools

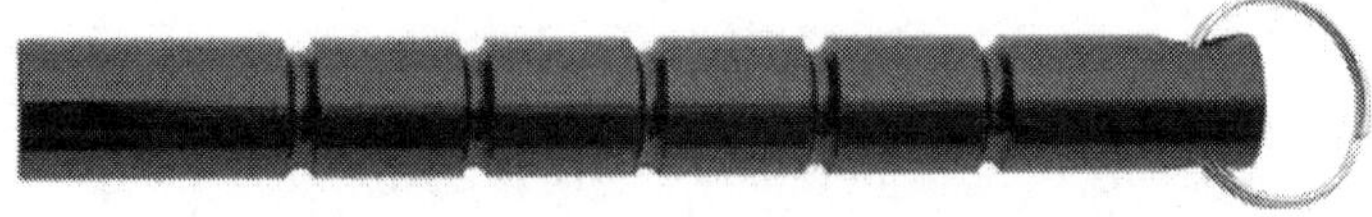

The Kubotan

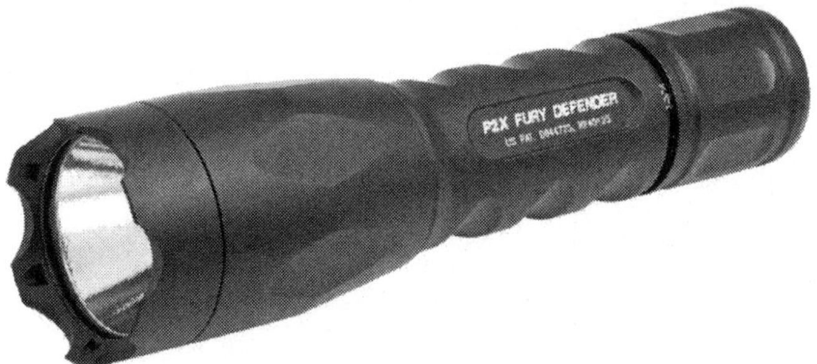

Tactical Flashlight

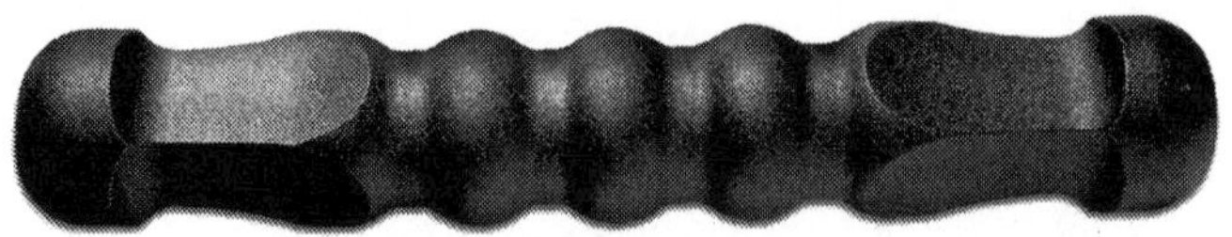

The Yawara

Pictured here, a kubotan used as a fist loading weapon.

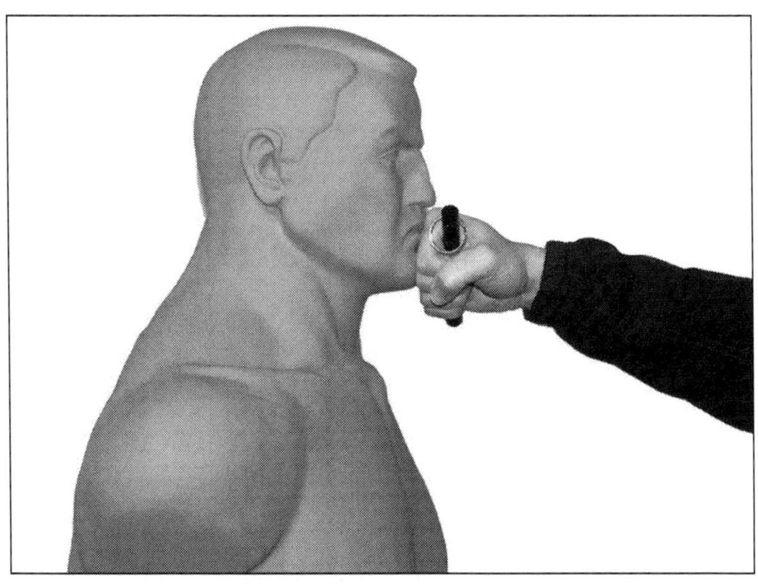

Fist loading techniques are best practiced on the body opponent bag.

Fist Loading Concealment

Concealing your fist loading weapon is of paramount importance. The following photo sequence demonstrates the proper way to conceal a kubotan prior to initiating a first strike.

The Push Over

Bullies love to push people around. In fact, pushing is often mistaken as a combat ritual when, in fact, it's a probe used to assess your reactions.

How you react to a chest or shoulder push is relevant because it provides a lot of valuable information to your adversary. When pushed, do you appear angry or frustrated, or confused and scared? Are you clumsy and fall to the floor? Do you appear strong, confident and in control of the situation? Are you angered easily? All of your nonverbal reactions to a simple push are essential to the knuckle-dragger's assessment and overall plan of attack.

The ***Push Over*** is similar to Pretend to be a Wimp except your goal is to passively accept the first push and retaliate when the opponent attempts a second one. By deceiving the adversary with erroneous reactions (feigning fright, weakness, clumsiness, and submission), you will misdirect his assessment, lower his guard, and lure him in for a devastating sucker punch.

As a general rule, pushing assaults are often conducted in a series and not just one isolated move. However, there is no guarantee that your adversary will attempt a second push. Some people are going to attack you right after they initiate the first push. Just be alert and prepared and always keep in mind that when you're dealing with human behavior, anything can happen.

The Push Over is not an "attack by draw" tactic and should only be used when the opponent has caught you off guard with his probing assault. Under no circumstances should you permit the opponent to get the upper hand by allowing him to attack you first.

Light Him Up

Light Him Up is a trick that falls under the category of strategic positioning. Here, your goal is to use the lighting in your environment to gain the advantage over the opponent.

When confronted by a threatening adversary, try to position yourself so that the immediate light source (the sun, auto headlights, street lamp, motion sensor lights, security lights, neon store signs, tactical flashlight, etc.) glares into his eyes and not yours. The instant the opponent squints his eyes or looks away, blindside him with a knockout punch.

Hand it Over

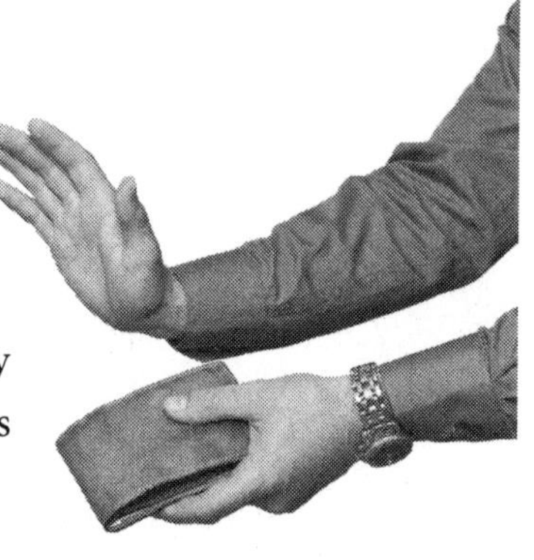

There's something about cash money that gives a would-be attacker pause for thought This deceptive technique is used when you're faced with a mugger demanding your money or some other valuable possession (this is assuming, of course, that he's not brandishing a weapon).

When the would-be thief steps into range and demands your valuables (i.e., wallet, watch, jewelry, car keys, cellphone), you should appear nervous, frightened, and conciliatory.

Hand it Over also works well with the Pretend to be a Wimp trick. Remember to be convincing, not dramatic.

Next, use your nondominant hand to give up the item (you'll want your strong dominant hand to be ready to attack). Just before the thief grabs hold of your item, let is slip out of your hand. When his eyes and immediate attention follow the descending object, slug him with all you've got!

The Shirt Grabber

This is a *reactive* sucker punch technique designed to counter the ever so popular shirt grab. Like the chest push, a shirt grab is another type of probing technique used to assess your reactions such as fear, anger, confidence, intimidation, etc.

The Shirt Grabber counter also works well with the Pretend to be a Wimp trick. Again, be convincing!

In most cases, if your adversary grabs your shirt, it's just a matter of seconds before he musters the confidence to slug you with his free hand. Therefore, it's best to counter toot sweet. Here's how to do it:

1. When the adversary grabs your shirt, maintain your balance with your feet spread apart and weight evenly distributed.
2. Keep control of your emotions - don't get angry.
3. Appear compliant, slowly raising your hands at chest level.
4. Use your mirror image hand (i.e., if the opponent grabs your with his right hand, use your left hand) to trap the opponent's grabbing hand against your chest.
5. Simultaneously counter with a sucker punch.

The Chest Poker

This sucker punch technique is almost identical to the Shirt Grabber move, except your adversary is poking you in the chest instead of grabbing your clothing.

Like the chest push and shirt grab, the chest poke is a just another type of probe or feeler used to assess your overall demeanor and level of confidence. However, like every *reactive* sucker punch technique, it's important to immediately counter the adversary before it's too late.

It's not uncommon for the opponent's finger to break when applying the Chest Poke counter. However, much will depend on the force of your trapping hand and the position of the opponent's finger.

Here's how to counter a chest poker:

1. When the adversary pokes your chest, maintain your balance with your feet spread apart and weight evenly distributed.
2. Keep control of your emotions - don't get angry or slap the opponent's hand away from your body. Remember, if you're not in control of your emotions, you are not in control of the situation.
3. Appear compliant by slowly raising your hands at the level of the chest poke.
4. Again, use your mirror image hand (i.e., if the opponent pokes your with his right hand, use your left hand) to trap the opponent's finger against your chest. Press hard so his hand is immobilized.
5. With your free hand, simultaneously counter with a sucker punch. The palm heel strike tends to work best.

Blindside Him

If you're lucky, there might come a time when you'll have the opportunity to blindside your adversary and attack him from the rear. From this vantage point, you with have two options: to strike him or choke him out.

If your goal is to hit your opponent, you can deliver a few strategically placed shots with his back to you. They include the base of the skull, the side of the face, and spine. However, remember that the base of the skull and spine are considered deadly force targets and should only be struck when deadly force is warranted and justified in the eyes of the law.

If your objective is to apply a rear standing choke, the rear naked choke technique will serve you well. Now, if you encounter a taller adversary, you'll need to lower him into the choke by simultaneously applying a cross over stomp kick.

The cross over stomp kick is deceptive, non telegraphic, and exceptionally fast, which means its difficult to see and counter. The kick is delivered with your rear leg and contact is made with the heel of your foot to the back of the opponent's knee.

Pictured here, the cross over stomp kick prior to delivering a rear choke.

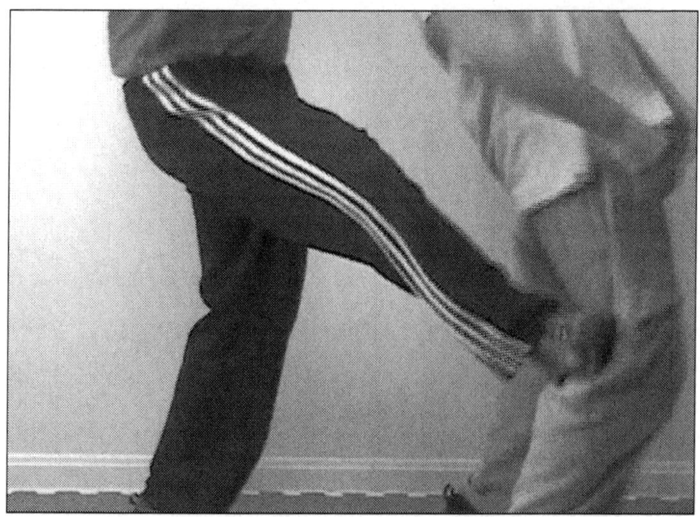

Close up of the cross over stomp kick

Chapter 7
Sucker Punch Training

What to Expect

In this chapter, I'm going to teach you specific drills and exercises for developing your sucker punching skills and then I will help you design a solid training program. Most of the suggestions in this chapter are the culmination of years of research, analysis, and experimentation. I have used these exercises to teach thousands of students over the past three decades and I'm confident they will help you in your training. Let's begin with some of the equipment you'll need in your training.

Sucker Punch Equipment Training

Equipment training is a vital component of sucker punch readiness. Let's start off with the body opponent bag.

The Body Opponent Bag

The body opponent bag (aka BOB) is, by far, the best piece of training equipment for developing *accurate* sucker punch techniques. Unlike the traditional heavy bag, this freestanding mannequin bag provides realistic facial targets that you can attack with full-speed, full-force strikes.

Accurate and powerful knockout punches take time and practice to master. Remember to start out slowly and progressively build up the speed and intensity of your strikes. If you are a beginner, avoid the urge to attack the bag with maximum speed and force. Take your time and enjoy the process of learning an invaluable new skill.

There's only one drawback to the body opponent bag and it's his head! When it comes to throwing powerful head shots, the body opponent bag has limitations. The head of the bag is light and flexible and cannot withstand power punching. It simply doesn't offer the resistance necessary for a serious heavy hitter.

That's not to say that you can't develop powerful kicks, punches, and strikes on the body opponent bag. You can! As a matter of fact, the torso of the body opponent bag provides tremendous resistance against powerful body shots and will give the most seasoned fighter a great workout. Just remember, the body opponent bag should be used for accuracy training, not power.

Realistic facial features makes the body opponent bag a great tool for developing accurate sucker punch techniques.

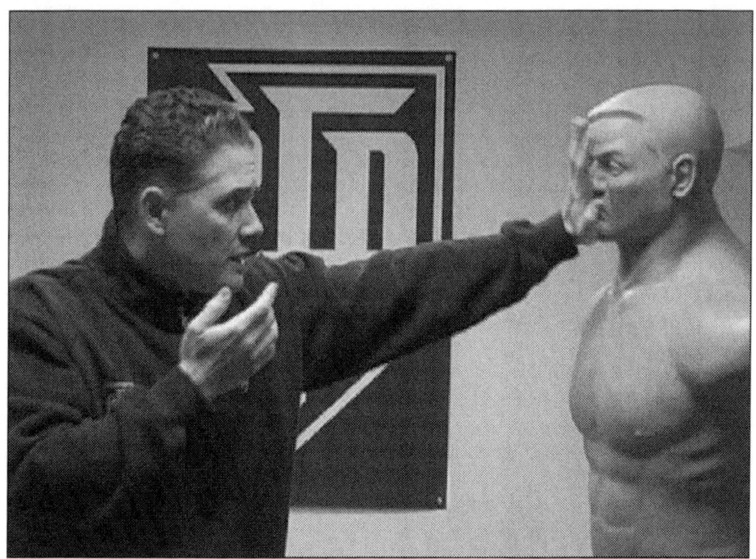

Sucker punch demonstration #1: Pictured here, the author demonstrates a palm heel strike on the body opponent bag.

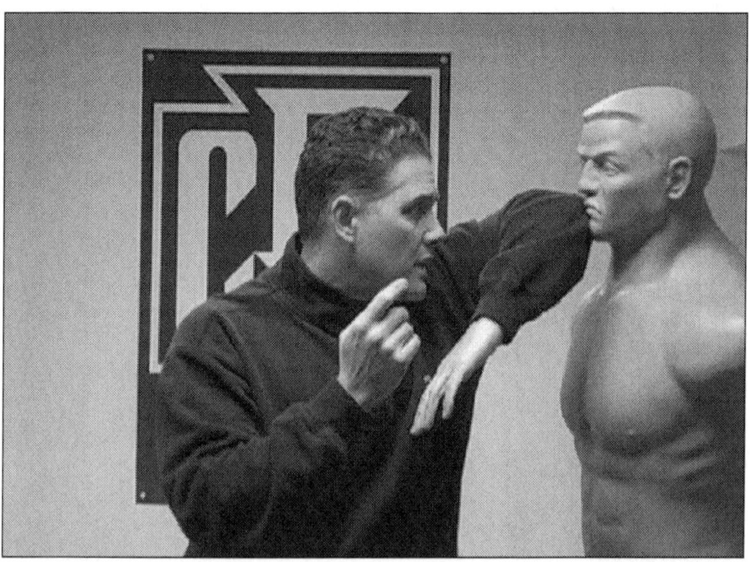

Sucker punch demonstration #2: Here, Sammy Franco performs an elbow strike on the body opponent bag.

Body Opponent Bag Training Tips

What follows is a list of tips to help maximize your training on the body opponent bag.

- Before you begin training, make certain that you have been cleared by your doctor. Since there is always some risk involved in training and because each person is unique, it is important that before beginning any type of training program, you should have a complete physical examination by your physician.
- Before hitting the bag, always warm up with some light stretching and calisthenics.
- Always start your first round on the bag with light punches and strikes. Never go all out in the beginning of your workout session.
- When hitting the bag, never sacrifice proper technique for power or speed.
- Always throw your sucker punch techniques from a solid stance.
- Don't chew gum when working out on the bag.
- Avoid wearing watches and jewelry when training.
- Never hold your breath. Remember to exhale with the delivery of every technique.
- Always be cognizant of your distance from the bag. Stand too close when punching the bag will result in a "pushing effect" while standing too far will just cause the punch to simply glance the target.
- Avoid the habit of tapping your gloves or fists together before delivering a punch.

- If you don't know the proper way to throw a punch, get instruction from a qualified coach or instructor.
- Avoid locking out your elbows when punching the bag.
- Avoid premature exhaustion by pacing yourself during your bag workouts.
- The body opponent bag doesn't hit back, so be aware of your own target openings and vulnerabilities when hitting the bag.
- Remember to always maintain your balance always when punching the bag - never sacrifice your balance for power.
- The body opponent bag can be unforgiving on your body and will certainly test the structural integrity of you punches and blows. Please remember to keep your wrists straight when your fists hit the bag. Learn to gradually build up the force of your blows - a beginner's wrists are generally too weak to accommodate full force strikes on the punching bag.
- When using the body opponent bag, learn to relax and avoid unnecessarily tensing your arm and shoulder muscles. Muscular tension will throw off the timing of your punches, retard the speed of your blows, kicks and strikes and most certainly wear you out during your workout.
- Punching bags often cause fighters to "lose their form" when delivering their blows. Try to be constantly aware of your form when hitting the bag or better yet have a training partner, teacher or coach observe you when working out on the bag. Another suggestion is to videotape yourself using the punching bag. This will give you a good idea of what you are doing in your workouts.
- Avoid bag training two days in a row. Give your body a few days to recover from your last workout.

- To avoid injury or burn out, don't engage in body opponent bag training more than three times per week.
- Get into the habit of regularly inspecting your bag for tears and other signs of wear.
- Stay hydrated when working out on the bag. Dehydration can have a real negative effect on your workout, and it can also be dangerous.

If you need to stabilize the face of the body opponent bag, you can have a training partner brace the back of its head.

The Heavy Bag

Heavy bag training is the number one tool for developing *powerful* sucker punch strikes. It also improves muscular endurance, strengthens bones, tendons, and ligaments, conditions the cardiovascular system, and helps channel aggressive energy.

The heavy bag is constructed of either top grain leather, canvas or vinyl. Most bags are 14 inches in diameter and 42 inches in length. The interior of the bag is filled with either cotton fiber, thick foam, sand or other durable material.

Depending on the brand, heavy bags can weigh anywhere from seventy-five to two hundred and fifty pounds. However, for our purposes, I suggest a bag that weighs a minimum of 150 pounds.

Safe and effective heavy bag training will require you to find a place that will allow both you and the bag to move around freely. The location should also be a relatively quiet place that is free of distractions. Here are a few places you might want to consider:

- Garage
- Carport
- Basement
- Barn
- Home gym
- Open field/backyard
- Warehouse
- Under a deck

Before you begin working out, invest in a good pair of bag gloves that will protect your hands when working out. When buying gloves, spare no expense and look for a reputable and high-quality brand. This will provide years of reliable use and will help ensure a better quality workout.

If you don't think you'll need bag gloves, think again. Striking the heavy bag without hand protection causes sore knuckles, bruised bones, hand inflammation, sore wrists and scraped knuckles. As a result, it will set your training back for several weeks in order for your hands to heal.

Focus Mitts

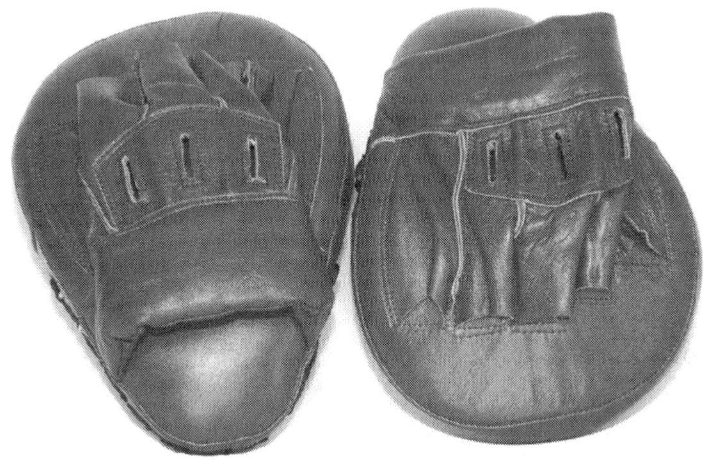

Focus mitts are great for developing both accurate and powerful first strike techniques. It also improves defensive skills, accuracy, speed, target recognition, target selection, target impact, and timing in all offensive techniques.

The focus mitt (also called punching mitt or focus pad) is an exceptional piece of training equipment that can be used by anyone. By placing the mitts at various angles and levels, you can perform every conceivable kick, punch, or strike known to mankind. Properly utilized, focus mitts will refine your defensive reaction time and condition your entire body for fighting.

Focus mitts are constructed of durable leather designed to withstand tremendous punishment. Compared to other pieces of equipment, the focus mitt is relatively inexpensive. However, an effective workout requires two mitts (one for each hand). Your training partner (called the feeder) plays a vital role in focus mitt workouts by controlling the techniques you execute and the cadence of delivery. The intensity of your workouts will depend largely upon his or her ability to manipulate the mitts and push you to your limit. I often tell my students that a good focus mitt feeder is one step ahead of his training partner, whereas a great focus mitt feeder is two steps ahead of his partner.

When training with your partner, give them constructive feedback and let them know how he or she is doing. Remember, communication is vital during your workout sessions. Also, try to avoid remaining stationary. Get into the habit of constantly moving around with quick, economical steps.

To truly benefit from any focus mitt workout, you must learn to concentrate intensely throughout the entire session. You must block out both internal and external distractions. Try to visualize the focus mitt as a living, breathing assailant, not an inanimate target. This type of visualization will make the difference between a poor workout and a great training session. You also might want to draw small Xs on the mitts. This practice will improve your focus and concentration and help you develop accurate sucker punch strikes.

The Training Methodologies

Before we move to the different sucker punch workout routines, it's important to talk about two important training methodologies. Essentially, all of the sucker punch routines presented in this section will fall under one of two different types of training methods; they are proficiency training and street training. Let's take a look at each one.

Proficiency Training

Proficiency Training is the staple of sucker punch training, and it's used to sharpen one specific punch or strike at a time by executing it over and over for a prescribed number of repetitions. Each time the sucker punch technique is performed with clean form at various speeds. Sucker punches are also carried out with the eyes closed to develop a kinesthetic feel for the action. Proficiency Training develops speed, power, accuracy, non-telegraphic movement, balance, and psychomotor skill.

Street Training

As I discussed earlier, the ultimate goal of a sucker punch is to quickly put an end to a fight with one knockout blow. However, you must have a backup plan and be prepared if your preemptive strike doesn't neutralize the opponent.

Street Training prepares you for a sucker punch situation gone bad. It's your back up plan, to end the altercation once and for all. Since most fights are explosive, lasting an average of 20 seconds, you must prepare for this possible scenario. This means delivering explosive and powerful compound attacks with vicious intent for approximately 20 seconds, resting one minute, and then repeating the process. Well-conditioned athletes can go longer. In fact, a few of my students are capable of performing the street training methodology uninterrupted for a full minute.

Street Training prepares you for the stress and immediate fatigue of a real fight. It also develops speed, power, explosiveness, target selection and recognition, timing, footwork, pacing, and breath control. You can also practice this methodology in different lighting, on different terrains, and in various environmental settings.

Designing a Great Sucker Punch Program

In this section, I'm going to show you how to design a sucker punch training program using the equipment and methodologies I discussed earlier. However, before we begin, you must be certain that your program meets the following criteria.

- **Realistic** - sucker punch training should be as real as possible. It should include drills and exercises that replicate real world scenarios and conditions.
- **Simple** - your training should be easy to put into action. It should not require time-consuming preparation or expensive equipment.
- **Specific** - your training should meet specific training goals. This might be a micro goal, such as improving a specific strike or mastering a particular sucker punch ruse. Avoid the urge to tackle everything at once. Instead, devote your attention to one skill at a time.
- **Stressful** - your training should be stressful (mentally and physically) so you will be prepared for the rigors of real fighting.
- **Quantifiable** - you must be able to accurately measure your progress in training. Performance measurement is motivational and helps you stay committed to your goals. It also useful for identifying methodologies that are not helping you reach your personal objectives.

Many Roads to the Same Destination

There's no single sucker punch program that works for everyone. Since each of us has different goals, and time lines, it's up to you to identify your needs and personalize your training accordingly. The bottom line is, *only you can determine what works best for you.*

There are many ways to set up a good training program. In fact, some of you might want to first consult with self-defense trainer prior to setting up a program and schedule.

Be Smart! Get a Check-Up First

Sucker punch training can be very taxing on your heart. So, before you begin any exercise program, including those suggested in this book, it is important to check with your doctor to see if you have any condition that might be aggravated by this type of strenuous exercise.

Warming Up

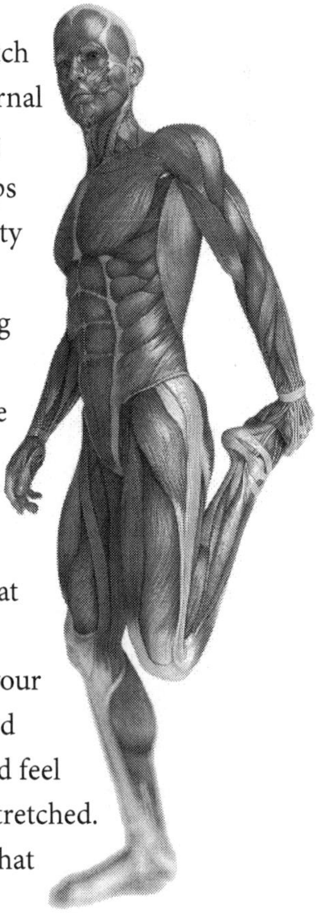

Before beginning any of the drills, it's important that you first warm up and stretch out. Warming up slowly increases the internal temperature of your body while stretching improves your workout performance, keeps you flexible, and helps reduce the possibility of an injury.

Some of the best exercises for warming up are jumping jacks, rope skipping or a short jog before training. Another effective method of warming up your muscles is to perform light and easy movements with the weights.

When stretching out, keep in mind that all movements should be performed in a slow and controlled manner. Try to hold your stretch for a minimum of sixty seconds and avoid all bouncing movements. You should feel mild tension on the muscle that is being stretched. Remember to stay relaxed and focus on what you are doing. Here are seven stretches to get you started.

- **Neck stretch** - from a comfortable standing position, slowly tilt your head to the right side of your neck, holding it for a count of twenty. Then tilt your head to the left side for approximately twenty seconds. Stretch each side of the neck at least three times.

- **Triceps stretch** - from a standing position, keep your knees slightly bent, extend your right arm overhead, hold the elbow of your right arm with your left hand, and slowly pull your right elbow to the left. Keep your hips straight as you stretch your triceps gently for thirty seconds. Repeat this stretch for the other arm.

- **Hamstring stretch** - from a seated position on the floor, extend your right leg in front of you with your toe pointing to the ceiling. Place the sole of your left foot in the inside of your extended leg. Gently lean forward at the hips and stretch out the hamstrings of your right leg. Hold this position for a minimum of sixty seconds. Switch legs and repeat the stretch.

- **Spinal twist** - from a seated position on the floor, extend your right leg in front of you. Raise your left leg and place it on the outside of your right leg. Place your right elbow on the outside of your left thigh. Stabilize your stretch with your elbow and twist your upper body and head to your left side. Breathe naturally and hold this stretch for a minimum of thirty seconds. Switch legs and repeat this stretch for the other side.

- **Quad stretch** - assume a sitting position on the floor with your hamstrings folded and resting on top of your calves. Your toes should be pointed behind you, and your instep should be flush with the ground. Sit comfortably into the stretch and hold for a minimum of sixty seconds.

- **Prone stretch** - lay on the ground with your back to the floor. Exhale as you straighten your arms and legs. Your fingers and toes should be stretching in opposite directions. Hold this stretch for thirty seconds.

- **Groin stretch** - sit on the ground with the soles of your feet touching each other. Grab hold of your feet and slowly pull yourself forward until mild tension is felt in your groin region. Hold this position for a minimum of sixty seconds.

Besides reducing the possibility of injury, stretching also improves circulation, promotes better posture, and relaxes your muscles.

Sucker Punch Drills and Exercises

The following drills are designed to develop both your sucker punch techniques and the secondary strikes you'll use in a compound attack.

While all of these exercises are demonstrated on a heavy bag, some of them can also be performed on the body opponent bag and focus mitts. Let's start with Technique Isolation Training.

Technique Isolation Training

Technique Isolation training is a form of proficiency training that can be used for both sucker punch and secondary strike techniques. The purpose of this exercise is to focus exclusively on one specific strike (i.e., finger jab, lead straight, rear cross, hook, uppercut, palm heel, etc.) for your entire workout. For example, if you want to sharpen and develop your lead straight punch (used for compound attacks), you would isolate and practice it exclusively on the heavy bag for a specified number of rounds.

Isolation Training (Lead Straight) Demonstration

Step 1: The practitioner assumes a fighting stance.

Step 2: He delivers a high lead straight at the bag.

Step 3: He begins circling the bag in a clockwise direction.

Step 4: He throws a low lead straight.

Step 5: As he moves around the bag, he throws another high punch.

Step 6: Next, another low punch.

Step 7: Followed by a high lead straight punch.

Step 8: He delivers another low punch and continues to circle around the heavy bag.

Step 9: He fires off another high punch.

Step 10: The practitioner continues punching and moving around the at the bag for a duration of 3 minutes.

Technique Isolation Workout Routines			
Skill Level	Duration of Each Round	Rest Period	Total Number of rounds
Beginner	1 minute	2 minutes	3
Beginner	1 minute	1 minute	3
Beginner	2 minutes	2 minutes	3
Beginner	2 minutes	1 minute	3
Intermediate	3 minutes	2 minutes	5
Intermediate	3 minutes	1 minute	5
Intermediate	3 minutes	2 minutes	6
Intermediate	3 minutes	1 minute	6
Advanced	4 minutes	2 minutes	8
Advanced	4 minutes	1 minute	8
Advanced	5 minutes	2 minutes	10
Advanced	5 minutes	1 minute	10

In order to maximize the full benefit of technique isolation training, it's important to stick to only one technique for your entire workout. For example, if you're a beginner who wants to perfect your uppercut punch, you would practice it exclusively for a total of 3 rounds.

Elevation Drill

If you are looking to develop knock-out punching power, look no further than the elevation drill. In fact, this is one of the most demanding exercises you can perform on the heavy bag. Besides requiring a tremendous amount of muscular endurance, the drill also requires a significant amount of mental resilience and attention control.

The objective of this exercise is to keep the heavy bag elevated at a 45-degree angle by continuously punching it. Warning! This drill is brutal on the arms. In fact, the average person can barely last 30 seconds. To perform the drill follow these steps:

1. Face the heavy bag and assume a fighting stance.
2. Deliver the lead straight and rear cross combination continuously. Concentrate on delivering full-speed, full-force punches.
3. Maintain a rapid-fire cadence to keep the bag elevated at a

45-degree angle from the floor.

4. Avoid pushing the bag and remember to snap each blow. If the heavy bag spins when performing this exercise, it means your punches are not landing at the center of the bag. Remember to focus your blows at a single target point.

5. Perform the drill for a minimum of three rounds. Each round can last anywhere from 10 to 90 seconds. If you are exceptionally conditioned, go for 90 seconds.

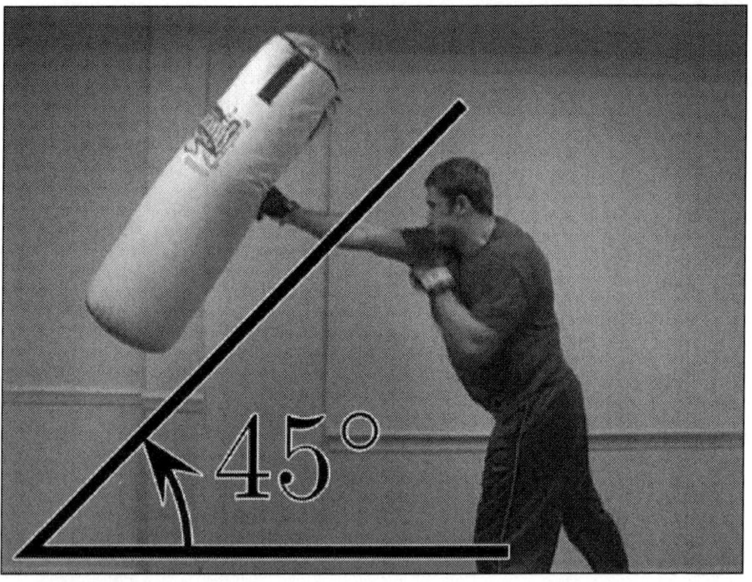

The goal of the elevation drill is to keep the heavy bag elevated at approximately 45-degrees by continuously punching it.

Be very careful when performing this exercise. One misplaced punch or bent wrist can easily lead to a severe injury.

Elevation Drill Demonstration

Step 1: The practitioner assumes a fighting stance.

Step 2: He begins with a powerful lead straight punch.

Step 3: He immediately follows with a rear cross.

Step 4: Next, another lead straight punch.

Step 5: The speed and power of the blows elevate the heavy bag at a 45-degree angle.

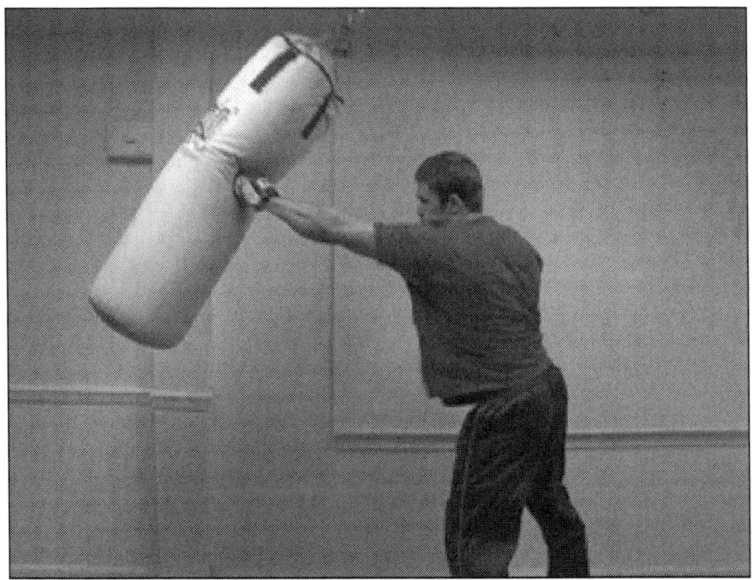

Step 6: To keep the bag elevated at 45-degrees, the practitioner must continue to attack the heavy bag with vicious intent.

Step 7: The practitioner delivers another rapid-fire rear across.

Step 8: Followed by another powerful lead punch.

Step 9: The practitioner continues his barrage for a total of 60 seconds.

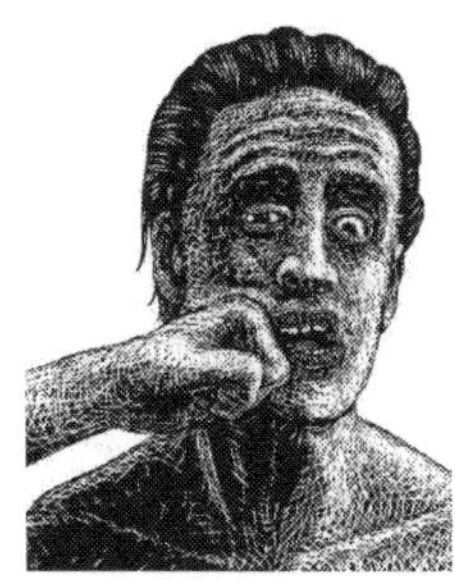

While the elevation drill is strictly designed for developing linear punching power, it's also a great methodology for developing mental toughness.

Elevation Drill Workout Routines

Skill Level	Duration of Each Round	Rest Period	Total Number of rounds
Beginner	10 seconds	2 minutes	3
Beginner	15 seconds	1 minute	3
Beginner	20 seconds	2 minutes	3
Beginner	25 minutes	1 minute	3
Intermediate	30 seconds	2 minutes	5
Intermediate	35 seconds	1 minute	5
Intermediate	40 seconds	2 minutes	5
Intermediate	45 seconds	1 minute	5
Advanced	60 seconds	2 minutes	6
Advanced	70 seconds	1 minute	6
Advanced	80 seconds	2 minutes	6
Advanced	90 seconds	1 minute	6

Cyclone Drill

The Cyclone Drill develops is designed to develop bone-crushing hook punches. The objective of the exercise is to assault the heavy bag with a continuous flurry of hook punches delivered in a back and forth fashion. This drill also permits you to strike both high and low heavy bag targets. To perform the Cyclone drill, follow these steps:

1. Face the heavy bag and assume a fighting stance.
2. Deliver the lead and rear hook punches in a fluid, back and forth fashion. Concentrate on striking the bag as fast and hard as possible.
3. Perform the drill for a minimum of three rounds. Each round can last anywhere from 10 to 90 seconds.

Cyclone Drill Demonstration

Step 1: The practitioner throws a high lead hook punch at the bag.

Step 2: Next, a rear hook.

Step 3: Followed by a lead hook.

Step 4: He continues with a rear hook.

Step 5: Then another high lead hook punch.

Step 6: The practitioner continues his assault for a total of 30 seconds.

Cyclone Drill Workout Routines

Skill Level	Duration of Each Round	Rest Period	Total Number of rounds
Beginner	10 seconds	2 minutes	3
Beginner	15 seconds	1 minute	3
Beginner	20 seconds	2 minutes	3
Beginner	25 minutes	1 minute	3
Intermediate	30 seconds	2 minutes	5
Intermediate	35 seconds	1 minute	5
Intermediate	40 seconds	2 minutes	5
Intermediate	45 seconds	1 minute	5
Advanced	60 seconds	2 minutes	6
Advanced	70 seconds	1 minute	6
Advanced	80 seconds	2 minutes	6
Advanced	90 seconds	1 minute	6

"Punch-a Hole" Exercise

Any fighter worth his salt will tell you that heavy bag training is a delicate mixture of power, speed, timing, and pacing. However, the real secret to making it through a full three-minute round on the heavy bag is to pace the power of your strikes.

Some of you might already know that full force, full speed punching will invariably lead to a very short-lived training round. In most instances, the average person can only sustain "all out" power punching for approximately 30 seconds. That's also assuming they are punching with proper form.

The "Punch a Hole" exercise goes against this conventional wisdom by training you to hit the bag as hard as humanly possible. In essence, your goal is to literally try and punch a hole through the heavy bag. Is this actually possible? I seriously doubt it! Nevertheless, this type of training will transform your fists into virtual sledgehammers.

"Punch a Hole" Workout Demonstration

Step 1: The practitioner assumes a fighting stance.

Step 2: He throws a rear cross punch.

Step 3: Next, he follows up with a strong lead straight punch.

Step 4: He drives a powerful low rear uppercut.

Step 5: A high lead hook punch.

Step 6: Followed by a bone-shattering rear cross.

Step 7: Another explosive lead punch.

Step 8: The practitioner continues his assault for a total of 30 seconds.

Beginner Level
"Punch a Hole" Workout Routines

Workout Routine	Duration of Each Round	Rest Period	Total Number of rounds
1	10 seconds	2 minutes	3
2	10 seconds	1 minute	3
3	15 seconds	2 minutes	3
4	15 seconds	1 minute	3
5	20 seconds	2 minutes	3
6	20 seconds	1 minute	3
7	25 seconds	2 minutes	3
8	25 seconds	1 minute	3
9	10 seconds	1 minute	5
10	15 seconds	2 minutes	5
11	20 seconds	1 minute	5
12	25 seconds	2 minutes	5

The "punch a hole" drill requires you to hit the bag as hard as possible! Do not perform this exercise unless you are absolutely certain you have mastered the proper body mechanics of punching.

Intermediate Level
"Punch a Hole" Workout Routines

Workout Routine	Duration of Each Round	Rest Period	Total Number of rounds
1	30 seconds	2 minutes	3
2	30 seconds	1 minute	3
3	35 seconds	2 minutes	3
4	35 seconds	1 minute	3
5	40 seconds	2 minutes	3
6	40 seconds	1 minute	3
7	45 seconds	2 minutes	3
8	45 seconds	1 minute	3
9	30 seconds	1 minute	5
10	35 seconds	2 minutes	5
11	40 seconds	1 minute	5
12	45 seconds	2 minutes	5

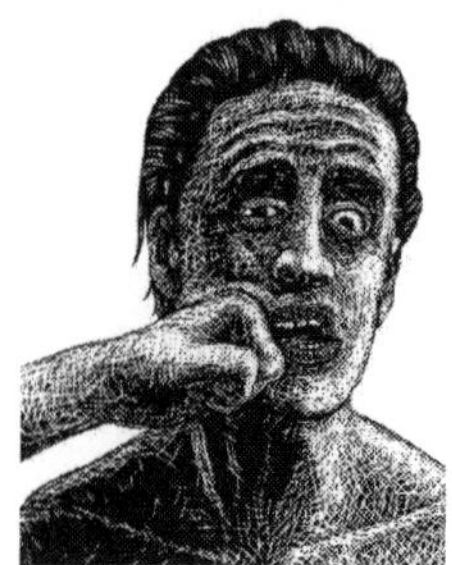

Performing this drill for a duration of 30-45 seconds might not seem like a lot. However, I can assure you that after 5 rounds you will be thoroughly exhausted.

Advanced Level
"Punch a Hole" Workout Routines

Workout Routine	Duration of Each Round	Rest Period	Total Number of rounds
1	50 seconds	2 minutes	4
2	50 seconds	1 minute	4
3	55 seconds	2 minutes	4
4	55 seconds	1 minute	4
5	60 seconds	2 minutes	5
6	60 seconds	1 minute	5
7	65 seconds	2 minutes	5
8	65 seconds	1 minute	5
9	50 seconds	1 minute	6
10	55 seconds	2 minutes	6
11	60 seconds	1 minute	6
12	65 seconds	2 minutes	6

Performing this drill for a duration of 60 seconds or longer is generally reserved for professional fighters who want peak combat performance.

Disingenuous Vocalization Exercises

One of the most important attributes for effective sucker punching is the ability to speak calmly and strike simultaneously. Here are four effective vocalization exercises that will help you develop this deceptive and indispensable fighting skill.

The Pledge Drill

This exercise requires that you verbally recite the Pledge of Allegiance of the United States. While you are reciting the pledge your training partner is to yell, "Attack!" and you are to immediately launch a preselected compound attack in the air. The key is to deliver a devastating sucker punch while continuing to recite the pledge in a calm and controlled manner. It's critical that you do not alter the tone, pitch, volume, or tempo of your voice when delivering your assault.

Nursery Rhyme Drill (Beginner level)

This exercise is similar to the pledge drill except that it requires you to verbally recite a simple children's nursery rhyme, such as "Mary Had a Little Lamb" or "Hickory, Dickory, Dock." Once again, while you are reciting the rhyme, your training partner yells, "Attack!" and you are to immediately launch a preselected compound attack in the air without disturbing the vocalization of the rhyme. Once again, it's critical not to alter the tonality of your voice when delivering your assault.

Tongue Twister (Intermediate level)

The tongue twister is an intermediate-level drill that requires you to slowly and repeatedly recite a tongue twister, such as "She sells seashells on the seashore of Seychelles" or "Peter Piper picked a peck of pickled peppers." While you are reciting this statement, your training partner is to yell, "Attack!" and you must immediately launch a preselected compound attack in the air. Once again, it's critical that you do not disturb the vocalization or alter the tone, pitch, volume, or tempo of your voice when delivering your assault.

The Alphabet Drill (Advanced level)

The Alphabet exercise is a more advanced drill. Your objective here is to slowly recite the alphabet backward. At some point during your recitation, your training partner is to yell, "Attack!" and you are to immediately launch a preselected compound attack in the air while continuing to recite the alphabet backwards. Don't get frustrated with this exercise; it's designed to challenge you.

Hand Conditioning

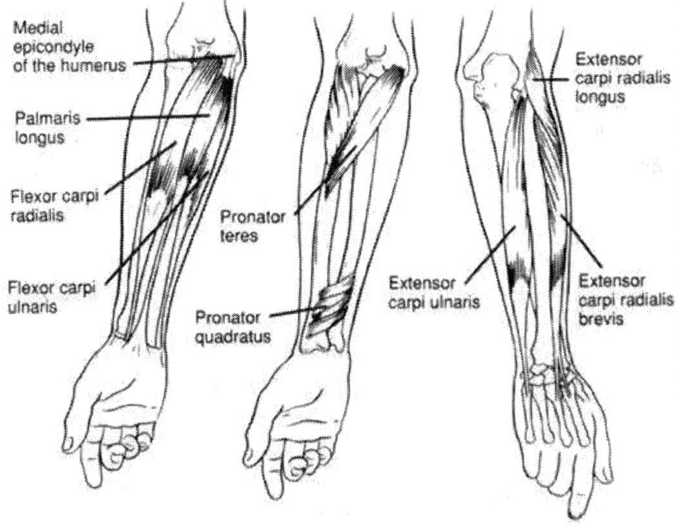

It's no surprise that strong fingers, wrists and forearms will significantly enhance punching power. Powerful hands and forearms will amplify the power of your strikes and help ensure a single knockout hit. There are several effective hand and forearm exercises you can perform to strengthen these muscles.

What follows are several ways to condition and strengthen your hands, wrists and forearms.

Power Putty

One excellent hand exerciser that strengthens all the muscles in your fingers and hands is Power Putty. Essentially, Power Putty is a flexible silicone rubber that can be squeezed, stretched, and crushed. Begin using the putty for ten minute sessions and progressively build up to thirty minutes.

This tough resistant putty will strengthen the muscles of your forearm, wrists, hands and fingers. Remember to work both hands equally.

Hand Grippers

Another effective way to strengthen your hands, wrists and forearms is to work out with heavy duty hand grippers. While there are a wide selection of them on the market, I personally prefer using the Captains of Crush brand. These high quality grippers are virtually indestructible and they are sold in a variety of different resistance levels ranging from 60 to 365 pounds.

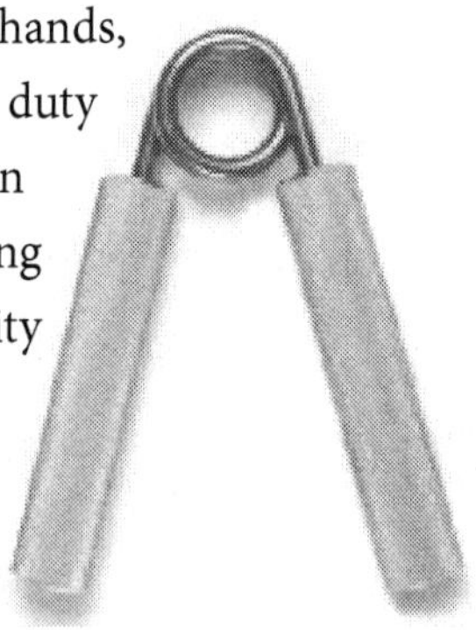

Tennis Ball

If you are low on cash and just starting out with your training, you can begin by squeezing a tennis ball a couple times per week. One hundred repetitions per hand would be a great start.

Weight Training

Finally, you can also condition your wrists and forearms by performing various forearm exercises with free weights. Exercises like: hammer curls, reverse curls, wrist curls, and reverse wrist curls are great for developing powerful forearms. When training your forearms, be certain to work both your extensor and flexor muscles. Let's look at some of the exercises.

Barbell Wrist Curls

This exercise strengthens the flexor muscles. Perform 5 sets of 8-10 repetitions. To perform the exercise, follow these steps:

1. Sit at the end of a bench, grab a barbell with an underhand grip and place both of your hands close together.
2. In a smooth and controlled fashion, slowly bend your wrists and lower the barbell toward the floor.
3. Contract your forearms and curl the weight back to the starting position.

Reverse Wrist Curls

This exercise develops and strengthens the extensor muscle of the forearm. Perform 6 sets of 6-8 repetitions. To perform the exercise, follow these steps:

1. Sit at the end of a bench, hold a barbell with an overhand grip (your hands should be approximately 11 inches apart) and place your forearms on top of your thighs.
2. Slowly lower the barbell as far as your wrists will allow.
3. Flex your wrists upward back to the starting position.

Behind-the-Back Wrist Curls

This exercise strengthens both the flexor muscles of the forearms. Perform 5 sets of 6-8 repetitions To perform the exercise, follow these steps:

1. Hold a barbell behind your back at arm's length (your hands

should be approximately shoulder-width apart).

2. Uncurl your finger and let the barbell slowly roll down your palms.
3. Close your hands and roll the barbell back into your hands.

Hammer Curls

This exercise strengthens both the Brachialis and Brachioradialis muscles. Perform 5 sets of 8-10 repetitions. To perform the exercise, follow these steps:

1. Stand with both feet approximately shoulder width apart, with both dumbbells at your sides.
2. Keeping your elbows close to your body and your palms facing inward, slowly curl both dumbbells upward towards your shoulders.
3. Slowly return to the starting position.

Reverse Barbell Curls

Reverse curls can be a great alternative to hammer curls. This exercise strengthens both the Brachialis and Brachioradialis muscles. Perform 5 sets of 8-10 repetitions. To perform the exercise, follow these steps:

1. Stand with both feet approximately shoulder width apart. Hold a barbell with your palms facing down (pronated grip).
2. Keeping your upper arms stationary, curl the weights up until the bar is at shoulder level.
3. Slowly return to the starting position.

General Fitness and Combat Conditioning

Finally, if you want to maximize the efficiency and effectiveness of your fighting skills, you must be physically fit. Fitness and conditioning comprises the following three broad components: cardiorespiratory conditioning, muscular/skeletal conditioning, and proper body composition.

The cardiorespiratory system includes the heart, lungs, and circulatory system, which undergo tremendous stress in a high-risk situation. So you're going to have to run, jog, bike, swim, or skip rope to develop sound cardiorespiratory conditioning. Each aerobic workout should last a minimum of 30 minutes and be performed at least four times per week.

The second component of conditioning is muscular/skeletal conditioning. To strengthen your bones and muscles to withstand the rigors of combat, your training must include progressive resistance (weight training). You will also need a stretching program designed to loosen up every muscle group. As I said earlier, stretching on a regular basis will also increase the muscles' range of motion, improve circulation, reduce the possibility of injury and relieve daily stress.

The final component of conditioning is proper body composition: simply, the ratio of fat to lean body tissue. Your diet and training regimen will affect your level or percentage of body fat significantly. A sensible and consistent exercise program accompanied by a healthy and balanced diet will facilitate proper body composition.

Finding the Right Training Partner

Many of these exercises can be performed individually, while others will require the assistance of a training partner or instructor.

A good training partner should motivate, challenge and push you to your limits. He or she doesn't have to share the same goals as you do, but they must be willing to help you reach your full potential. Your training partner or coach should also be somewhat familiar with the various fighting drills and equipment. For example, they should know how to hold and manipulate the focus mitts or perform sucker punch simulation drills.

While a good training partner can be a major asset, having a bad one can be a major liability. Be exceptionally careful who you choose to train with you. When looking for a training parter, try to avoid the following personality types:

1. **The conversationalist** - someone who talks too much and often disrupts the training intensity.
2. **The challenger** - someone who is naturally argumentative and tries to test your knowledge and patience.
3. **The ego tripper** - someone who will do anything to prove just how tough he is. He usually enjoys full-contact drills and likes to injure others in training.
4. **The insecure one** - someone who is hesitant to participate in training full-contact drills and exercises.
5. **The know-it-all** - someone who thinks he knows anything and everything about combat training.
6. **The dilettante** - someone who doesn't understand the importance of sucker punch training, and therefore doesn't fully commit himself to the program.

Finally, remember that a good training partner or coach is there to evaluate your performance during your workouts. Listen carefully to what he has to say. A good coach, for example, will be brutally honest and tell you what you are doing correctly and what you are doing wrong. Learn to put your ego aside and heed his advice.

Safety When Training

Safety precautions must always be taken when engaged in sucker punch training. Remember, a serious injury can set you back for weeks and even months. Don't make the mistake of letting your ego or laziness get the best of you. Learn to be safety-conscious. Here are a few suggestions to help minimize the possibilities of injury when training:

1. Buy the best training equipment that you can afford.
2. Know the proper way to use training equipment.
3. Regularly inspect your equipment for wear and defects.
4. Avoid ego-driven training partners or teachers.
5. Be especially aware when training with someone of superior size, skill, or experience.
6. Always warm up before training.
7. Drink plenty of water during training sessions to avoid dehydration.
8. Be cautious when performing training drills for the first time.

It's also a good idea to have a first-aid kit nearby. A first-aid kit is intended for both minor and major injuries. The kit should be kept in a well-sealed box away from children. Don't forget to write down the emergency number for your local hospital or medical clinic on the box. Most first-aid kits can be purchased at your local drugstore. Each kit should contain cotton wool and hydrogen peroxide for cleaning cuts, tweezers, scissors, triangular bandages, alcohol swabs, adhesive tape, adhesive bandages, antibiotic ointment, sterile pads, gauze bandages, and elastic bandages for sprains and for elbow and knee injuries.

Avoiding Overtraining & Burnout

Burnout is defined as a negative emotional state acquired by physical overtraining. Some symptoms of burnout include physical illness, boredom, anxiety, disinterest in training, and general sluggish behavior. Whether you are a beginner or expert, you're susceptible to burnout. Here are a few suggestions to help avoid burnout in your training:

1. Make your workouts intense but enjoyable.
2. Vary your training routine (i.e., hard day/easy day routine).
3. Pace yourself during your workouts - don't try to do it all in one day.
4. Listen to your body- if you don't feel up to training, skip a day.
5. Work out in different types of environments.
6. Use different types of training equipment.
7. Workout with different training partners.
8. Keep accurate records of your training routine.
9. Vary the intensity of your training throughout your workout.

Keeping Track of Your Training

In order to reap the full benefits of training, you need to keep track of your workouts and monitor your progress. Monitoring your training will give you a wide range of benefits, including:

1. Help determine if you making progress in your training.
2. The ability to effectively alter your training program.
3. Track your rate of progress,
4. Stay interested and motivated.
5. Break through performance plateaus.

Two of the best tools for keeping track of your training progress are: the training journal and video footage. Let's take a look at each one.

The Training Journal

Record keeping is one of the most important aspects of training. Try to make it a habit to keep accurate records of your workouts in a personal journal. This type of record keeping is important for some of the following reasons:

1. It will help you monitor your progress.
2. It will keep you organized.
3. It will inspire, motivate and remind you to stick to your goals.
4. It helps prevent potential injuries.
5. It will help you guard against over training.
6. If you are learning new skills, it accelerates the learning process.
7. It gives you valuable training information that can be analyzed.
8. It helps you determine which drills, activities, and exercises are unproductive.
9. It helps you determine which activities are helpful and productive.

10. When making entries into your journal, don't forget to include some of the following important details:

- The date and time you trained.
- The sucker punch skill set or attribute you are training.
- The types of drills and exercises you performed.
- The number or sets, reps you performed for each exercise or drill.
- The number or rounds and minutes per round you performed for each drill or exercise.
- The feelings you experienced before, during, and after your workout.
- Your overall mood.
- Concerns you have about your current training.
- Comments, ideas and observations made by your coach, training partner or instructor.

Videotaping

If you really want to actually see your progress, videotape your workouts. The video will provide you with a more accurate picture of what you are doing in your training. You will be able to observe mistakes and recognize your strengths and weaknesses. The video footage will also motivate you to train harder. Remember to date each videotape or video clip; later on you will be able to compare and see marked improvements in your training performance.

NOTES

Glossary

A

accuracy—The precise or exact projection of force. Accuracy is also defined as the ability to execute a combative movement with precision and exactness.

adaptability—The ability to physically and psychologically adjust to new or different conditions or circumstances of combat.

advanced first-strike tools—Offensive techniques that are specifically used when confronted with multiple opponents.

aerobic exercise—Literally, "with air." Exercise that elevates the heart rate to a training level for a prolonged period of time, usually 30 minutes.

affective preparedness – One of the three components of preparedness. Affective preparedness means being emotionally, philosophically, and spiritually prepared for the strains of combat. See cognitive preparedness and psychomotor preparedness.

aggression—Hostile and injurious behavior directed toward a person.

aggressive response—One of the three possible counters when assaulted by a grab, choke, or hold from a standing position. Aggressive response requires you to counter the enemy with destructive blows and strikes. See moderate response and passive response.

aggressive hand positioning—Placement of hands so as to imply aggressive or hostile intentions.

agility—An attribute of combat. One's ability to move his or her body quickly and gracefully.

amalgamation—A scientific process of uniting or merging.

ambidextrous—The ability to perform with equal facility on both the right and left sides of the body.

anabolic steroids – synthetic chemical compounds that resemble the male sex hormone testosterone. This performance-enhancing drug is known to increase lean muscle mass, strength, and endurance.

analysis and integration—One of the five elements of CFA's mental component. This is the painstaking process of breaking down various elements, concepts, sciences, and disciplines into their atomic parts, and then methodically and strategically analyzing, experimenting, and drastically modifying the information so that it fulfills three combative requirements: efficiency, effectiveness, and safety. Only then is it finally integrated into the CFA system.

anatomical striking targets—The various anatomical body targets that can be struck and which are especially vulnerable to potential harm. They include: the eyes, temple, nose, chin, back of neck, front of neck, solar plexus, ribs, groin, thighs, knees, shins, and instep.

anchoring – The strategic process of trapping the assailant's neck or limb in order to control the range of engagement during razing.

assailant—A person who threatens or attacks another person.

assault—The threat or willful attempt to inflict injury upon the person of another.

assault and battery—The unlawful touching of another person without justification.

assessment—The process of rapidly gathering, analyzing, and accurately evaluating information in terms of threat and danger. You can assess people, places, actions, and objects.

attack—Offensive action designed to physically control, injure, or kill another person.

attitude—One of the three factors that determine who wins a street fight. Attitude means being emotionally, philosophically, and spiritually liberated from societal and religious mores. See skills and knowledge.

attributes of combat—The physical, mental, and spiritual qualities that enhance combat skills and tactics.

awareness—Perception or knowledge of people, places, actions, and objects. (In CFA, there are three categories of tactical awareness: criminal awareness, situational awareness, and self-awareness.)

B

balance—One's ability to maintain equilibrium while stationary or moving.

blading the body—Strategically positioning your body at a 45-degree angle.

blitz and disengage—A style of sparring whereby a fighter moves into a range of combat, unleashes a strategic compound attack, and then quickly disengages to a safe distance. Of all sparring methodologies, the blitz and disengage most closely resembles a real street fight.

block—A defensive tool designed to intercept the assailant's attack by placing a non-vital target between the assailant's strike and your vital body target.

body composition—The ratio of fat to lean body tissue.

body language—Nonverbal communication through posture, gestures, and facial expressions.

body mechanics—Technically precise body movement during the execution of a body weapon, defensive technique, or other fighting maneuver.

body tackle – A tackle that occurs when your opponent haphazardly rushes forward and plows his body into yours.

body weapon—Also known as a tool, one of the various body parts that can be used to strike or otherwise injure or kill a criminal assailant.

burn out—A negative emotional state acquired by physically over- training. Some symptoms include: illness, boredom, anxiety, disinterest in training, and general sluggishness.

C

cadence—Coordinating tempo and rhythm to establish a timing pattern of movement.

cardiorespiratory conditioning—The component of physical fitness that deals with the heart, lungs, and circulatory system.

centerline—An imaginary vertical line that divides your body in half and which contains many of your vital anatomical targets.

choke holds—Holds that impair the flow of blood or oxygen to the brain.

circular movements—Movements that follow the direction of a curve.

close-quarter combat—One of the three ranges of knife and bludgeon combat. At this distance, you can strike, slash, or stab your assailant with a variety of close-quarter techniques.

cognitive development—One of the five elements of CFA's mental component. The process of developing and enhancing your fighting skills through specific mental exercises and techniques. See analysis and integration, killer instinct, philosophy, and strategic/tactical development.

cognitive exercises—Various mental exercises used to enhance fighting skills and tactics.

cognitive preparedness – One of the three components of preparedness. Cognitive preparedness means being equipped with the strategic concepts, principles, and general knowledge of combat. See affective preparedness and psychomotor preparedness.

combat-oriented training—Training that is specifically related to the harsh realities of both armed and unarmed combat. See ritual-oriented training and sport-oriented training.

combative arts—The various arts of war. See martial arts.

combative attributes—See attributes of combat.

combative fitness—A state characterized by cardiorespiratory and muscular/skeletal conditioning, as well as proper body composition.

combative mentality—Also known as the killer instinct, this is a combative state of mind necessary for fighting. See killer instinct.

combat ranges—The various ranges of unarmed combat.

combative utility—The quality of condition of being combatively useful.

combination(s)—See compound attack.

common peroneal nerve—A pressure point area located approximately four to six inches above the knee on the midline of the outside of the thigh.

composure—A combative attribute. Composure is a quiet and focused mind-set that enables you to acquire your combative agenda.

compound attack—One of the five conventional methods of attack. Two or more body weapons launched in strategic succession whereby the fighter overwhelms his assailant with a flurry of full speed, full-force blows.

conditioning training—A CFA training methodology requiring the practitioner to deliver a variety of offensive and defensive combinations for a 4-minute period. See proficiency training and street training.

contact evasion—Physically moving or manipulating your body to avoid being tackled by the adversary.

Contemporary Fighting Arts—A modern martial art and self-defense system made up of three parts: physical, mental, and spiritual.

conventional ground-fighting tools—Specific ground-fighting techniques designed to control, restrain, and temporarily incapacitate your adversary. Some conventional ground fighting tactics include: submission holds, locks, certain choking techniques, and specific striking techniques.

coordination—A physical attribute characterized by the ability to perform a technique or movement with efficiency, balance, and accuracy.

counterattack—Offensive action made to counter an assailant's initial attack.

courage—A combative attribute. The state of mind and spirit that enables a fighter to face danger and vicissitudes with confidence, resolution, and bravery.

creatine monohydrate—A tasteless and odorless white powder that mimics some of the effects of anabolic steroids. Creatine is a safe body-building product that can benefit anyone who wants to increase their strength, endurance, and lean muscle mass.

criminal awareness—One of the three categories of CFA awareness. It involves a general understanding and knowledge of the nature and dynamics of a criminal's motivations, mentalities, methods, and capabilities to perpetrate violent crime. See situational awareness and self-awareness.

criminal justice—The study of criminal law and the procedures associated with its enforcement.

criminology—The scientific study of crime and criminals.

cross-stepping—The process of crossing one foot in front of or behind the other when moving.

crushing tactics—Nuclear grappling-range techniques designed to crush the assailant's anatomical targets.

cue word - a unique word or personal statement that helps focus your attention on the execution of a skill, instead of its outcome.

D

deadly force—Weapons or techniques that may result in unconsciousness, permanent disfigurement, or death.

deception—A combative attribute. A stratagem whereby you delude your assailant.

decisiveness—A combative attribute. The ability to follow a tactical course of action that is unwavering and focused.

defense—The ability to strategically thwart an assailant's attack (armed or unarmed).

defensive flow—A progression of continuous defensive responses.

defensive mentality—A defensive mind-set.

defensive reaction time—The elapsed time between an assailant's physical attack and your defensive response to that attack. See offensive reaction time.

demeanor—A person's outward behavior. One of the essential factors to consider when assessing a threatening individual.

diet—A lifestyle of healthy eating.

disingenuous vocalization—The strategic and deceptive

utilization of words to successfully launch a preemptive strike at your adversary.

distancing—The ability to quickly understand spatial relationships and how they relate to combat.

distractionary tactics—Various verbal and physical tactics designed to distract your adversary.

double end bag—A small bag hung from the ceiling and anchored to the floor with two elastic cords. This unique training bag develops striking accuracy, speed, fighting rhythm, timing, eye-hand coordination, footwork and overall defensive skills.

double-leg takedown—A takedown that occurs when your opponent shoots for both of your legs to force you to the ground.

E

ectomorph—One of the three somatotypes. A body type characterized by a high degree of slenderness, angularity, and fragility. See endomorph and mesomorph.

effectiveness—One of the three criteria for a CFA body weapon, technique, tactic, or maneuver. It means the ability to produce a desired effect. See efficiency and safety.

efficiency—One of the three criteria for a CFA body weapon, technique, tactic, or maneuver. It means the ability to reach an objective quickly and economically. See effectiveness and safety.

emotionless—A combative attribute. Being temporarily devoid of human feeling.

endomorph—One of the three somatotypes. A body type characterized by a high degree of roundness, softness, and body fat. See ectomorph and mesomorph.

evasion—A defensive maneuver that allows you to strategically maneuver your body away from the assailant's strike.

evasive sidestepping—Evasive footwork where the practitioner moves to either the right or left side.

evasiveness—A combative attribute. The ability to avoid threat or danger.

excessive force—An amount of force that exceeds the need for a particular event and is unjustified in the eyes of the law.

experimentation—The painstaking process of testing a combative hypothesis or theory.

explosiveness—A combative attribute that is characterized by a sudden outburst of violent energy.

F

fear—A strong and unpleasant emotion caused by the anticipation or awareness of threat or danger. There are three stages of fear in order of intensity: fright, panic, and terror. See fright, panic, and terror.

feeder—A skilled technician who manipulates the focus mitts.

femoral nerve—A pressure point area located approximately 6 inches above the knee on the inside of the thigh.

fighting stance—Any one of the stances used in CFA's system. A strategic posture you can assume when face-to-face with an unarmed assailant(s). The fighting stance is generally used after you have launched your first-strike tool.

fight-or-flight syndrome—A response of the sympathetic nervous system to a fearful and threatening situation, during which it prepares your body to either fight or flee from the perceived danger.

finesse—A combative attribute. The ability to skillfully execute a movement or a series of movements with grace and refinement.

first strike—Proactive force used to interrupt the initial stages of an assault before it becomes a self-defense situation.

first-strike principle—A CFA principle that states that when physical danger is imminent and you have no other tactical option but to fight back, you should strike first, strike fast, and strike with authority and keep the pressure on.

first-strike stance—One of the stances used in CFA's system. A strategic posture used prior to initiating a first strike.

first-strike tools—Specific offensive tools designed to initiate a preemptive strike against your adversary.

fisted blows – Hand blows delivered with a clenched fist.

five tactical options – The five strategic responses you can make in a self-defense situation, listed in order of increasing level of resistance: comply, escape, de-escalate, assert, and fight back.

flexibility—The muscles' ability to move through maximum natural ranges. See muscular/skeletal conditioning.

focus mitts—Durable leather hand mitts used to develop and sharpen offensive and defensive skills.

footwork—Quick, economical steps performed on the balls of the feet while you are relaxed, alert, and balanced. Footwork is structured around four general movements: forward, backward, right, and left.

fractal tool—Offensive or defensive tools that can be used in more than one combat range.

fright—The first stage of fear; quick and sudden fear. See panic and terror.

full Beat – One of the four beat classifications in the Widow Maker Program. The full beat strike has a complete initiation and retraction phase.

G

going postal - a slang term referring to a person who suddenly and unexpectedly attacks you with an explosive and frenzied flurry of blows. Also known as postal attack.

grappling range—One of the three ranges of unarmed combat. Grappling range is the closest distance of unarmed combat from which you can employ a wide variety of close-quarter tools and techniques. The grappling range of unarmed combat is also divided into two planes: vertical (standing) and horizontal (ground fighting). See kicking range and punching range.

grappling-range tools—The various body tools and techniques that are employed in the grappling range of unarmed combat, including head butts; biting, tearing, clawing, crushing, and gouging tactics; foot stomps, horizontal, vertical, and diagonal elbow strikes, vertical and diagonal knee strikes, chokes, strangles, joint locks, and holds. See punching range tools and kicking range tools.

ground fighting—Also known as the horizontal grappling plane, this is fighting that takes place on the ground.

guard—Also known as the hand guard, this refers to a fighter's hand positioning.

guard position—Also known as leg guard or scissors hold, this is a ground-fighting position in which a fighter is on his back holding his opponent between his legs.

H

half beat – One of the four beat classifications in the Widow Maker Program. The half beat strike is delivered through the retraction phase of the proceeding strike.

hand positioning—See guard.

hand wraps—Long strips of cotton that are wrapped around the hands and wrists for greater protection.

haymaker—A wild and telegraphed swing of the arms executed by an unskilled fighter.

head-hunter—A fighter who primarily attacks the head.

heavy bag—A large cylindrical bag used to develop kicking, punching, or striking power.

high-line kick—One of the two different classifications of a kick. A kick that is directed to targets above an assailant's waist level. See low-line kick.

hip fusing—A full-contact drill that teaches a fighter to "stand his ground" and overcome the fear of exchanging blows with a stronger opponent. This exercise is performed by connecting two fighters with a 3-foot chain, forcing them to fight in the punching range of unarmed combat.

histrionics—The field of theatrics or acting.

hook kick—A circular kick that can be delivered in both kicking and punching ranges.

hook punch—A circular punch that can be delivered in both the punching and grappling ranges.

I

impact power—Destructive force generated by mass and velocity.

impact training—A training exercise that develops pain tolerance.

incapacitate—To disable an assailant by rendering him unconscious or damaging his bones, joints, or organs.

initiative—Making the first offensive move in combat.

inside position—The area between the opponent's arms, where he has the greatest amount of control.

intent—One of the essential factors to consider when assessing a threatening individual. The assailant's purpose or motive. See demeanor, positioning, range, and weapon capability.

intuition—The innate ability to know or sense something without the use of rational thought.

J

jersey Pull – Strategically pulling the assailant's shirt or jacket over his head as he disengages from the clinch position.

joint lock—A grappling-range technique that immobilizes the assailant's joint.

K

kick—A sudden, forceful strike with the foot.

kicking range—One of the three ranges of unarmed combat. Kicking range is the furthest distance of unarmed combat wherein you use your legs to strike an assailant. See grappling range and punching range.

kicking-range tools—The various body weapons employed in the kicking range of unarmed combat, including side kicks, push kicks, hook kicks, and vertical kicks.

killer instinct—A cold, primal mentality that surges to your consciousness and turns you into a vicious fighter.

kinesics—The study of nonlinguistic body movement communications. (For example, eye movement, shrugs, or facial gestures.)

kinesiology—The study of principles and mechanics of human movement.

kinesthetic perception—The ability to accurately feel your body during the execution of a particular movement.

knowledge—One of the three factors that determine who will win a street fight. Knowledge means knowing and understanding how to fight. See skills and attitude.

L

lead side -The side of the body that faces an assailant.

leg guard—See guard position.

linear movement—Movements that follow the path of a straight line.

low-maintenance tool—Offensive and defensive tools that require the least amount of training and practice to maintain proficiency. Low maintenance tools generally do not require preliminary stretching.

low-line kick—One of the two different classifications of a kick. A kick that is directed to targets below the assailant's waist level. (See high-line kick.)

lock—See joint lock.

M

maneuver—To manipulate into a strategically desired position.

MAP—An acronym that stands for moderate, aggressive, passive. MAP provides the practitioner with three possible responses to various grabs, chokes, and holds that occur from a standing position. See aggressive response, moderate response, and passive response.

Marathon des Sables (MdS) - a six-day, 156-mile ultramarathon held in southern Morocco, in the Sahara Desert. It is considered by many to be the toughest footrace on earth.

martial arts—The "arts of war."

masking—The process of concealing your true feelings from your opponent by manipulating and managing your body language.

mechanics—(See body mechanics.)

mental toughness - a performance mechanism utilizing a collection of mental attributes that allow a person to cope, perform and prevail through the stress of extreme adversity.

mental component—One of the three vital components of the CFA system. The mental component includes the cerebral aspects of fighting including the killer instinct, strategic and tactical development, analysis and integration, philosophy, and cognitive development. See physical component and spiritual component.

mesomorph—One of the three somatotypes. A body type classified by a high degree of muscularity and strength. The mesomorph possesses the ideal physique for unarmed combat. See ectomorph and endomorph.

mobility—A combative attribute. The ability to move your body quickly and freely while balanced. See footwork.

moderate response—One of the three possible counters when assaulted by a grab, choke, or hold from a standing position. Moderate response requires you to counter your opponent with a control and restraint (submission hold). See aggressive response and passive response.

modern martial art—A pragmatic combat art that has evolved to meet the demands and characteristics of the present time.

mounted position—A dominant ground-fighting position where a fighter straddles his opponent.

muscular endurance—The muscles' ability to perform the same

motion or task repeatedly for a prolonged period of time.

muscular flexibility—The muscles' ability to move through maximum natural ranges.

muscular strength—The maximum force that can be exerted by a particular muscle or muscle group against resistance.

muscular/skeletal conditioning—An element of physical fitness that entails muscular strength, endurance, and flexibility.

N

naked choke—A throat choke executed from the chest to back position. This secure choke is executed with two hands and it can be performed while standing, kneeling, and ground fighting with the opponent.

neck crush – A powerful pain compliance technique used when the adversary buries his head in your chest to avoid being razed.

neutralize—See incapacitate.

neutral zone—The distance outside the kicking range at which neither the practitioner nor the assailant can touch the other.

nonaggressive physiology—Strategic body language used prior to initiating a first strike.

nontelegraphic movement—Body mechanics or movements that do not inform an assailant of your intentions.

nuclear ground-fighting tools—Specific grappling range tools designed to inflict immediate and irreversible damage. Nuclear tools and tactics include biting tactics, tearing tactics, crushing tactics, continuous choking tactics, gouging techniques, raking tactics, and all striking techniques.

O

offense—The armed and unarmed means and methods of attacking a criminal assailant.

offensive flow—Continuous offensive movements (kicks, blows, and strikes) with unbroken continuity that ultimately neutralize or terminate the opponent. See compound attack.

offensive reaction time—The elapsed time between target selection and target impaction.

one-mindedness—A state of deep concentration wherein you are free from all distractions (internal and external).

ostrich defense—One of the biggest mistakes one can make when defending against an opponent. This is when the practitioner looks away from that which he fears (punches, kicks, and strikes). His mentality is, "If I can't see it, it can't hurt me."

P

pain tolerance—Your ability to physically and psychologically withstand pain.

panic—The second stage of fear; overpowering fear. See fright and terror.

parry—A defensive technique: a quick, forceful slap that redirects an assailant's linear attack. There are two types of parries: horizontal and vertical.

passive response—One of the three possible counters when assaulted by a grab, choke, or hold from a standing position. Passive response requires you to nullify the assault without injuring your adversary. See aggressive response and moderate response.

patience—A combative attribute. The ability to endure and

tolerate difficulty.

perception—Interpretation of vital information acquired from your senses when faced with a potentially threatening situation.

philosophical resolution—The act of analyzing and answering various questions concerning the use of violence in defense of yourself and others.

philosophy—One of the five aspects of CFA's mental component. A deep state of introspection whereby you methodically resolve critical questions concerning the use of force in defense of yourself or others.

physical attributes—The numerous physical qualities that enhance your combative skills and abilities.

physical component—One of the three vital components of the CFA system. The physical component includes the physical aspects of fighting, such as physical fitness, weapon/technique mastery, and combative attributes. See mental component and spiritual component.

physical conditioning—See combative fitness.

physical fitness—See combative fitness.

positional asphyxia—The arrangement, placement, or positioning of your opponent's body in such a way as to interrupt your breathing and cause unconsciousness or possibly death.

positioning—The spatial relationship of the assailant to the assailed person in terms of target exposure, escape, angle of attack, and various other strategic considerations.

postal attack - see going postal.

power—A physical attribute of armed and unarmed combat. The amount of force you can generate when striking an anatomical target.

power generators—Specific points on your body that generate

impact power. There are three anatomical power generators: shoulders, hips, and feet.

precision—See accuracy.

preemptive strike—See first strike.

premise—An axiom, concept, rule, or any other valid reason to modify or go beyond that which has been established.

preparedness—A state of being ready for combat. There are three components of preparedness: affective preparedness, cognitive preparedness, and psychomotor preparedness.

probable reaction dynamics - The opponent's anticipated or predicted movements or actions during both armed and unarmed combat.

proficiency training—A CFA training methodology requiring the practitioner to execute a specific body weapon, technique, maneuver, or tactic over and over for a prescribed number of repetitions. See conditioning training and street training.

proxemics—The study of the nature and effect of man's personal space.

proximity—The ability to maintain a strategically safe distance from a threatening individual.

pseudospeciation—A combative attribute. The tendency to assign subhuman and inferior qualities to a threatening assailant.

psychological conditioning—The process of conditioning the mind for the horrors and rigors of real combat.

psychomotor preparedness—One of the three components of preparedness. Psychomotor preparedness means possessing all of the physical skills and attributes necessary to defeat a formidable adversary. See affective preparedness and cognitive preparedness.

punch—A quick, forceful strike of the fists.

punching range—One of the three ranges of unarmed combat. Punching range is the mid range of unarmed combat from which the fighter uses his hands to strike his assailant. See kicking range and grappling range.

punching-range tools—The various body weapons that are employed in the punching range of unarmed combat, including finger jabs, palm-heel strikes, rear cross, knife-hand strikes, horizontal and shovel hooks, uppercuts, and hammer-fist strikes. See grappling-range tools and kicking-range tools.

Q

qualities of combat—See attributes of combat.

quarter beat - One of the four beat classifications of the Widow Maker Program. Quarter beat strikes never break contact with the assailant's face. Quarter beat strikes are primarily responsible for creating the psychological panic and trauma when Razing.

R

range—The spatial relationship between a fighter and a threatening assailant.

range deficiency—The inability to effectively fight and defend in all ranges of combat (armed and unarmed).

range manipulation—A combative attribute. The strategic manipulation of combat ranges.

range proficiency—A combative attribute. The ability to effectively fight and defend in all ranges of combat (armed and unarmed).

ranges of engagement—See combat ranges.

ranges of unarmed combat—The three distances (kicking range, punching range, and grappling range) a fighter might physically engage with an assailant while involved in unarmed combat.

raze – To level, demolish or obliterate.

razer – One who performs the Razing methodology.

razing – The second phase of the Widow Maker Program. A series of vicious close quarter techniques designed to physically and psychologically extirpate a criminal attacker.

razing amplifier - a technique, tactic or procedure that magnifies the destructiveness of your razing technique.

reaction dynamics—see probable reaction dynamics.

reaction time—The elapsed time between a stimulus and the response to that particular stimulus. See offensive reaction time and defensive reaction time.

rear cross—A straight punch delivered from the rear hand that crosses from right to left (if in a left stance) or left to right (if in a right stance).

rear side—The side of the body furthest from the assailant. See lead side.

reasonable force—That degree of force which is not excessive for a particular event and which is appropriate in protecting yourself or others.

refinement—The strategic and methodical process of improving or perfecting.

relocation principle—Also known as relocating, this is a street-fighting tactic that requires you to immediately move to a new location (usually by flanking your adversary) after delivering a compound attack.

repetition—Performing a single movement, exercise, strike, or action continuously for a specific period.

research—A scientific investigation or inquiry.

rhythm—Movements characterized by the natural ebb and flow of related elements.

ritual-oriented training—Formalized training that is conducted without intrinsic purpose. See combat-oriented training and sport-oriented training.

S

safety—One of the three criteria for a CFA body weapon, technique, maneuver, or tactic. It means that the tool, technique, maneuver or tactic provides the least amount of danger and risk for the practitioner. See efficiency and effectiveness.

scissors hold—See guard position.

scorching – Quickly and inconspicuously applying oleoresin capsicum (hot pepper extract) on your fingertips and then razing your adversary.

self-awareness—One of the three categories of CFA awareness. Knowing and understanding yourself. This includes aspects of yourself which may provoke criminal violence and which will promote a proper and strong reaction to an attack. See criminal awareness and situational awareness.

self-confidence—Having trust and faith in yourself.

self-enlightenment—The state of knowing your capabilities, limitations, character traits, feelings, general attributes, and motivations. See self-awareness.

set—A term used to describe a grouping of repetitions.

shadow fighting—A CFA training exercise used to develop and

refine your tools, techniques, and attributes of armed and unarmed combat.

sharking – A counter attack technique that is used when your adversary grabs your razing hand.

shielding wedge - a defensive maneuver used to counter an unarmed postal attack.

situational awareness—One of the three categories of CFA awareness. A state of being totally alert to your immediate surroundings, including people, places, objects, and actions. (See criminal awareness and self-awareness.)

skeletal alignment—The proper alignment or arrangement of your body. Skeletal alignment maximizes the structural integrity of striking tools.

skills—One of the three factors that determine who will win a street fight. Skills refers to psychomotor proficiency with the tools and techniques of combat. See Attitude and Knowledge.

slipping—A defensive maneuver that permits you to avoid an assailant's linear blow without stepping out of range. Slipping can be accomplished by quickly snapping the head and upper torso sideways (right or left) to avoid the blow.

snap back—A defensive maneuver that permits you to avoid an assailant's linear and circular blows without stepping out of range. The snap back can be accomplished by quickly snapping the head backward to avoid the assailant's blow.

somatotypes—A method of classifying human body types or builds into three different categories: endomorph, mesomorph, and ectomorph. See endomorph, mesomorph, and ectomorph.

sparring—A training exercise where two or more fighters fight each other while wearing protective equipment.

speed—A physical attribute of armed and unarmed combat. The rate or a measure of the rapid rate of motion.

spiritual component—One of the three vital components of the CFA system. The spiritual component includes the metaphysical issues and aspects of existence. See physical component and mental component.

sport-oriented training—Training that is geared for competition and governed by a set of rules. See combat-oriented training and ritual-oriented training.

sprawling—A grappling technique used to counter a double- or single-leg takedown.

square off—To be face-to-face with a hostile or threatening assailant who is about to attack you.

stance—One of the many strategic postures you assume prior to or during armed or unarmed combat.

stick fighting—Fighting that takes place with either one or two sticks.

strategic positioning—Tactically positioning yourself to either escape, move behind a barrier, or use a makeshift weapon.

strategic/tactical development—One of the five elements of CFA's mental component.

strategy—A carefully planned method of achieving your goal of engaging an assailant under advantageous conditions.

street fight—A spontaneous and violent confrontation between two or more individuals wherein no rules apply.

street fighter—An unorthodox combatant who has no formal training. His combative skills and tactics are usually developed in the street by the process of trial and error.

street training—A CFA training methodology requiring the

practitioner to deliver explosive compound attacks for 10 to 20 seconds. See condition ng training and proficiency training.

strength training—The process of developing muscular strength through systematic application of progressive resistance.

stress - physiological and psychological arousal caused by a stressor.

stressors - any activity, situation, circumstance, event, experience, or condition that causes a person to experience both physiological and psychological stress.

striking art—A combat art that relies predominantly on striking techniques to neutralize or terminate a criminal attacker.

striking shield—A rectangular shield constructed of foam and vinyl used to develop power in your kicks, punches, and strikes.

striking tool—A natural body weapon that impacts with the assailant's anatomical target.

strong side—The strongest and most coordinated side of your body.

style—The distinct manner in which a fighter executes or performs his combat skills.

stylistic integration—The purposeful and scientific collection of tools and techniques from various disciplines, which are strategically integrated and dramatically altered to meet three essential criteria: efficiency, effectiveness, and combative safety.

submission holds—Also known as control and restraint techniques, many of these locks and holds create sufficient pain to cause the adversary to submit.

sucker punch—Proactive force used to interrupt the initial stages of an assault before it becomes a self-defense situation. (See first strike.)

system—The unification of principles, philosophies, rules, strategies, methodologies, tools, and techniques of a particular method of combat.

T

tactic—The skill of using the available means to achieve an end.

target awareness—A combative attribute that encompasses five strategic principles: target orientation, target recognition, target selection, target impaction, and target exploitation.

target exploitation—A combative attribute. The strategic maximization of your assailant's reaction dynamics during a fight. Target exploitation can be applied in both armed and unarmed encounters.

target impaction—The successful striking of the appropriate anatomical target.

target orientation—A combative attribute. Having a workable knowledge of the assailant's anatomical targets.

target recognition—The ability to immediately recognize appropriate anatomical targets during an emergency self-defense situation.

target selection—The process of mentally selecting the appropriate anatomical target for your self-defense situation. This is predicated on certain factors, including proper force response, assailant's positioning, and range.

target stare—A form of telegraphing in which you stare at the anatomical target you intend to strike.

target zones—The three areas in which an assailant's anatomical targets are located. (See zone one, zone two and zone three.)

technique—A systematic procedure by which a task is

accomplished.

telegraphic cognizance—A combative attribute. The ability to recognize both verbal and non-verbal signs of aggression or assault.

telegraphing—Unintentionally making your intentions known to your adversary.

tempo—The speed or rate at which you speak.

terminate—To kill.

terror—The third stage of fear; defined as overpowering fear. See fright and panic.

timing—A physical and mental attribute of armed and unarmed combat. Your ability to execute a movement at the optimum moment.

tone—The overall quality or character of your voice.

tool—See body weapon.

traditional martial arts—Any martial art that fails to evolve and change to meet the demands and characteristics of its present environment.

traditional style/system—See traditional martial arts.

training drills—The various exercises and drills aimed at perfecting combat skills, attributes, and tactics.

trap and tuck - A counter move technique used when the adversary attempts to raze you during your quarter beat assault.

U

unified mind—A mind free and clear of distractions and focused on the combative situation.

use of force response—A combative attribute. Selecting the appropriate level of force for a particular self-defense situation.

V

viciousness—A combative attribute. The propensity to be extremely violent and destructive often characterized by intense savagery.

violence—The intentional utilization of physical force to coerce, injure, cripple, or kill.

visualization—Also known as mental visualization or mental imagery. The purposeful formation of mental images and scenarios in the mind's eye.

W

warm-up—A series of mild exercises, stretches, and movements designed to prepare you for more intense exercise.

weak side—The weaker and more uncoordinated side of your body.

weapon and technique mastery—A component of CFA's physical component. The kinesthetic and psychomotor development of a weapon or combative technique.

weapon capability—An assailant's ability to use and attack with a particular weapon.

webbing - The first phase of the Widow Maker Program. Webbing is a two hand strike delivered to the assailant's chin. It is called Webbing because your hands resemble a large web that wraps around the enemy's face.

widow maker – One who makes widows by destroying husbands.

widow maker program – A CFA combat program specifically designed to teach the law abiding citizen how to use extreme force when faced with immediate threat of unlawful deadly criminal attack. The Widow Maker program is divided into two phases or methodologies: Webbing and Razing.

Y

yell—A loud and aggressive scream or shout used for various strategic reasons.

Z

zero beat - One of the four beat classifications of the Widow Maker, Feral Fighting and Savage Street Fighting Programs. Zero beat strikes are full pressure techniques applied to a specific target until it completely ruptures. They include gouging, crushing, biting, and choking techniques.

zone one—Anatomical targets related to your senses, including the eyes, temple, nose, chin, and back of neck.

zone three—Anatomical targets related to your mobility, including thighs, knees, shins, and instep.

zone two—Anatomical targets related to your breathing, including front of neck, solar plexus, ribs, and groin.

About Sammy Franco

With over 30 years of experience, Sammy Franco is one of the world's foremost authorities on armed and unarmed self-defense. Highly regarded as a leading innovator in martial arts, Mr. Franco was one of the premier pioneers in the field of "reality-based" self-defense and combat instruction.

Sammy Franco is perhaps best known as the founder and creator of Contemporary Fighting Arts (CFA), a state-of-the-art offensive-based combat system that is specifically designed for real-world self-defense. CFA is a sophisticated and practical system of self-defense, designed specifically to provide efficient and effective methods to avoid, defuse, confront, and neutralize both armed and unarmed attackers.

Sammy Franco has frequently been featured in martial art magazines, newspapers, and appeared on numerous radio and television programs. Mr. Franco has also authored numerous books, magazine articles, and editorials and has developed a popular library of instructional videos.

Sammy Franco's experience and credibility in the combat science is unequaled. One of his many accomplishments in this field includes the fact that he has earned the ranking of a Law Enforcement Master Instructor, and has designed, implemented, and taught officer survival training to the United States Border Patrol (USBP). He has instructed members of the US Secret Service, Military Special Forces, Washington DC Police Department, Montgomery County, Maryland

Deputy Sheriffs, and the US Library of Congress Police. Sammy Franco is also a member of the prestigious International Law Enforcement Educators and Trainers Association (ILEETA) as well as the American Society of Law Enforcement Trainers (ASLET) and he is listed in the "Who's Who Director of Law Enforcement Instructors."

Sammy Franco is also a nationally certified Law Enforcement Instructor in the following curricula: PR-24 Side-Handle Baton, Police Arrest and Control Procedures, Police Personal Weapons Tactics, Police Power Handcuffing Methods, Police Oleoresin Capsicum Aerosol Training (OCAT), Police Weapon Retention and Disarming Methods, Police Edged Weapon Countermeasures and "Use of Force" Assessment and Response Methods.

Mr. Franco regularly conducts dynamic and enlightening seminars on different aspects of combat training, mental toughness and achieving personal peak performance.

On a personal level, Sammy Franco is an animal lover, who will go to great lengths to assist and rescue animals. Throughout the years, he's rescued everything from turkey vultures to goats. However, his most treasured moments are always spent with his beloved German Shepherd dogs.

For more information about Mr. Franco, you can visit his website at **SammyFranco.com** or follow him on Twitter **@RealSammyFranco**

Other Books by Sammy Franco

KUBOTAN POWER
Quick and Simple Steps to Mastering the Kubotan Keychain
by Sammy Franco

With over 290 photographs and step-by-step instructions, Kubotan Power is the authoritative resource for mastering this devastating self-defense weapon. In this one-of-a-kind book, world-renowned self-defense expert, Sammy Franco takes thirty years of real-world teaching experience and gives you quick, easy and practical kubotan techniques that can be used by civilians, law enforcement personnel, or military professionals. 8.5 x 5.5, paperback, 290 photos, illustrations, 204 pages.

FIRST STRIKE
End a Fight in Ten Seconds or Less!
by Sammy Franco

Learn how to stop any attack before it starts by mastering the art of the preemptive strike. First Strike gives you an easy-to-learn yet highly effective self-defense game plan for handling violent close-quarter combat encounters. First Strike will teach you instinctive, practical and realistic self-defense techniques that will drop any criminal attacker to the floor with one punishing blow. By reading this book and by practicing, you will learn the hard-hitting skills necessary to execute a punishing first strike and ultimately prevail in a self-defense situation. 8.5 x 5.5, paperback, photos, illustrations, 202 pages.

MAXIMUM DAMAGE
Hidden Secrets Behind Brutal Fighting Combination
by Sammy Franco

Maximum Damage teaches you the quickest ways to beat your opponent by exploiting his physical and psychological reactions in a fight. Learn how to stay two steps ahead of your adversary by knowing exactly how he will react to your strikes before they are delivered. In this unique book, self-defense expert Sammy Franco reveals his unique Probable Reaction Dynamic (PRD) fighting method. Probable reaction dynamics are both a scientific and comprehensive offensive strategy based on the positional theory of combat. Regardless of your style of fighting, PRD training will help you overpower your opponent by integrating your strikes into brutal fighting combinations that are fast, ferocious and final! 8.5 x 5.5, paperback, 240 photos, illustrations, 238 pages.

HEAVY BAG TRAINING

For Boxing, Mixed Martial Arts and Self-Defense
(Heavy Bag Training Series Book 1)

by Sammy Franco

The heavy bag is one of the oldest and most recognizable pieces of training equipment. It's used by boxers, mixed martial artists, self-defense practitioners, and fitness enthusiasts. Unfortunately, most people don't know how to use the heavy bag correctly. Heavy Bag Training teaches you everything you ever wanted to know about working out on the heavy bag. In this one-of-a-kind book, world-renowned self-defense expert Sammy Franco provides you with the knowledge, skills, and attitude necessary to maximize the training benefits of the bag. 8.5 x 5.5, paperback, photos, illus, 172 pages.

HEAVY BAG COMBINATIONS

The Ultimate Guide to Heavy Bag Punching Combinations
(Heavy Bag Training Series Book 2)

by Sammy Franco

Heavy Bag Combinations is the second book in Sammy Franco's best-selling Heavy Bag Training Series. This unique book is your ultimate guide to mastering devastating heavy bag punching combinations. With over 300+ photographs and detailed step-by-step instructions, Heavy Bag Combinations provides beginner, intermediate and advanced heavy bag workout combinations that will challenge you for the rest of your life! In fact, even the most experienced athlete will advance his fighting skills to the next level and beyond. 8.5 x 5.5, paperback, photos, illus, 248 pages.

THE COMPLETE BODY OPPONENT BAG BOOK

by Sammy Franco

In this one-of-a-kind book, Sammy Franco teaches you the many hidden training features of the body opponent bag that will improve your fighting skills and boost your conditioning. With detailed photographs, step-by-step instructions, and dozens of unique workout routines, The Complete Body Opponent Bag Book is the authoritative resource for mastering this lifelike punching bag. It covers stances, punching, kicking, grappling techniques, mobility and footwork, targets, fighting ranges, training gear, time based workouts, punching and kicking combinations, weapons training, grappling drills, ground fighting, and dozens of workouts. 8.5 x 5.5, paperback, 139 photos, illustrations, 206 pages.

INVINCIBLE

Mental Toughness Techniques for the Street, Battlefield and Playing Field

by Sammy Franco

Invincible is a treasure trove of battle-tested techniques and strategies for improving mental toughness in all aspects of life. It teaches you how to unlock the true power of your mind and achieve success in sports, fitness, high-risk professions, self-defense, and other peak performance activities. However, you don't have to be an athlete or warrior to benefit from this unique mental toughness book. In fact, the mental skills featured in this indispensable program can be used by anyone who wants to reach their full potential in life. 8.5 x 5.5, paperback, photos, illus, 250 pages.

THE WIDOW MAKER PROGRAM

Extreme Self-Defense for Deadly Force Situations

by Sammy Franco

The Widow Maker Program is a shocking and revolutionary fighting style designed to unleash extreme force when faced with the immediate threat of an unlawful deadly criminal attack. In this unique book, self-defense innovator Sammy Franco teaches you his brutal and unorthodox combat style that is virtually indefensible and utterly devastating. With over 250 photographs and detailed step-by-step instructions, The Widow Maker Program teaches you Franco's surreptitious Webbing and Razing techniques. When combined, these two fighting methods create an unstoppable force capable of destroying the toughest adversary. 8.5 x 5.5, paperback, photos, illus, 218 pages.

FERAL FIGHTING

Advanced Widow Maker Fighting Techniques

by Sammy Franco

In this sequel, Sammy Franco marches forward with cutting-edge concepts and techniques that will take your self-defense skills to entirely new levels of combat performance. Feral Fighting includes Franco's revolutionary Shielding Wedge technique. When used correctly, it transforms you into an unstoppable human meat grinder, capable of destroying any criminal adversary. Feral Fighting also teaches you the cunning art or Scorching. Learn how to convert your fingertips into burning torches that generate over 2 million scoville heat units causing excruciating pain and temporarily blindness. 8.5 x 5.5, paperback, photos, illustrations, 204 pages.

SAVAGE STREET FIGHTING
Tactical Savagery as a Last Resort

by Sammy Franco

In this revolutionary book, Sammy Franco reveals the science behind his most primal street fighting method. Savage Street Fighting is a brutal self-defense system specifically designed to teach the law-abiding citizen how to use "Tactical Savagery" when faced with the immediate threat of an unlawful deadly criminal attack. Savage Street Fighting is systematically engineered to protect you when there are no other self-defense options left! With over 300 photographs and detailed step-by-step instructions, Savage Street Fighting is a must-have book for anyone concerned about real world self-defense. Now is the time to learn how to unleash your inner beast! 8.5 x 5.5, paperback, 317 photos, illustrations, 232 pages.

WAR MACHINE
How to Transform Yourself Into A Vicious & Deadly Street Fighter

by Sammy Franco

War Machine is a book that will change you for the rest of your life! When followed accordingly, War Machine will forge your mind, body and spirit into iron. Once armed with the mental and physical attributes of the War Machine, you will become a strong and confident warrior that can handle just about anything that life may throw your way. In essence, War Machine is a way of life. Powerful, intense, and hard. 11 x 8.5, paperback, photos, illustrations, 210 pages.

CONTEMPORARY FIGHTING ARTS, LLC

"Real World Self-Defense Since 1989"

SammyFranco.com

Printed in Great Britain
by Amazon